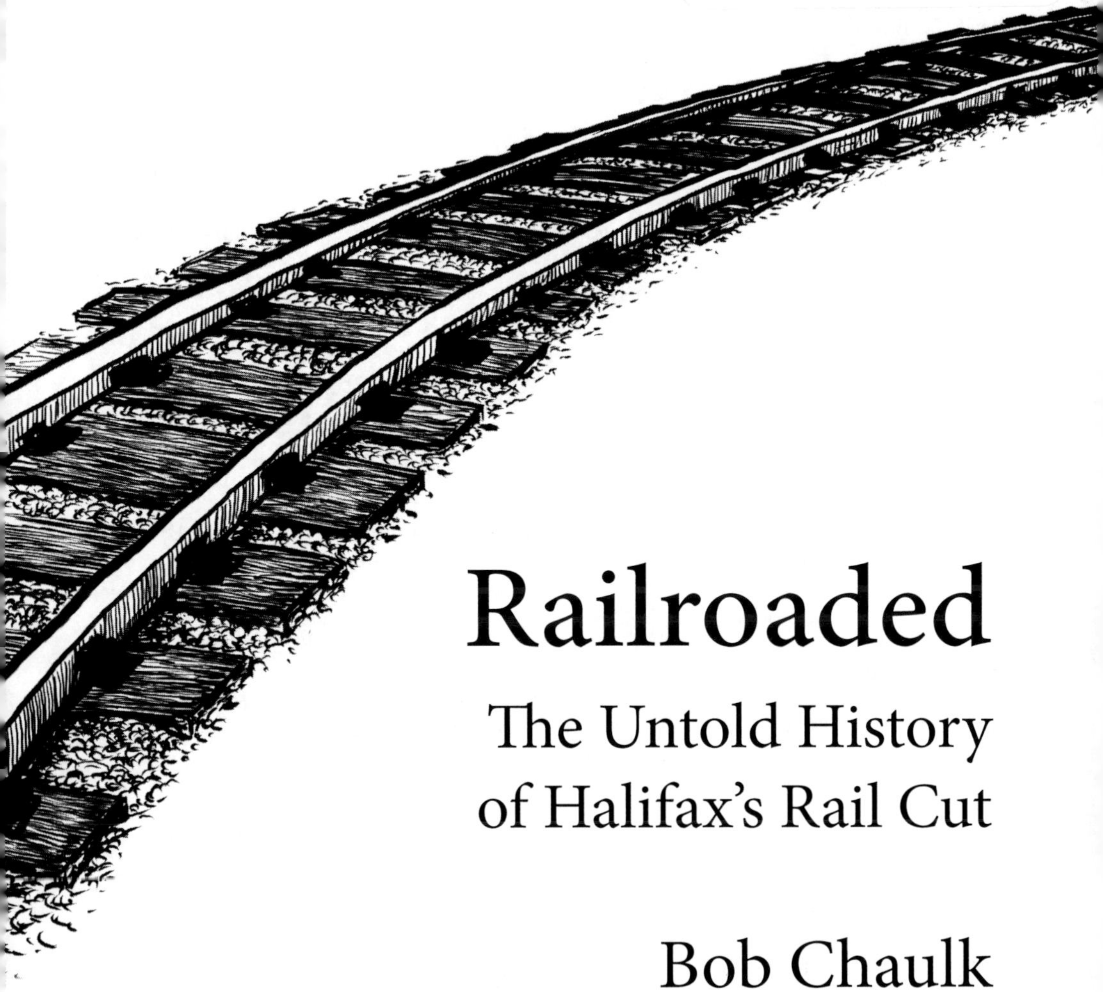

Railroaded

The Untold History of Halifax's Rail Cut

Bob Chaulk

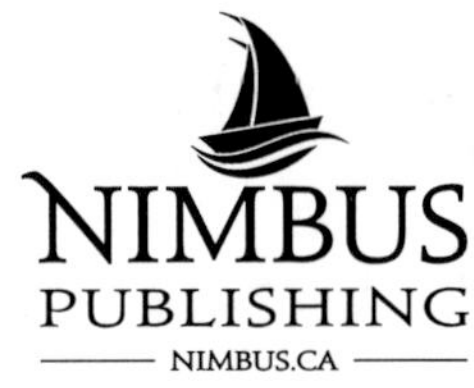
NIMBUS PUBLISHING
NIMBUS.CA

Nimbus Publishing Limited

3660 Strawberry Hill Street, Halifax, NS, B3K 5A9
(902) 455-4286 • nimbus.ca

Nimbus Publishing is based in Kjipuktuk, Mi'kma'ki, the traditional territory of the Mi'kmaq People.

Printed and bound in Canada
NB1764

MIX
Paper | Supporting responsible forestry
FSC® C013916
FSC www.fsc.org

Editor: Angela Mombourquette
Cover design: Heather Bryan; Railroad track illustration: Bee Stanton
Cover, above: The railway cut under construction at Young Avenue in March 1916. [Tom Lynskey collection]
Cover, below: Pier 2 in the 1930s. [Naval Museum of Halifax]
Interior design: Bee Stanton

Library and Archives Canada Cataloguing in Publication

Title: Railroaded : the untold history of Halifax's rail cut / Bob Chaulk.
Names: Chaulk, Bob, author
Description: Includes bibliographical references.
Identifiers: Canadiana (print) 20250218666 | Canadiana (ebook) 20250224860 | ISBN 9781774714775 (softcover) | ISBN 9781774714782 (EPUB)
Subjects: LCSH: Railroads—Nova Scotia—Halifax—Design and construction—History—20th century. | LCSH: Railroads—Nova Scotia—Halifax—Design and construction—History—20th century—Pictorial works. | LCSH: Railroads and state—Nova Scotia—Halifax—History—20th century. | LCSH: Railroads—Social aspects—Nova Scotia—Halifax—History—20th century. | LCSH: Halifax (N.S.)—History—20th century.
Classification: LCC HE2809.H35 C43 2025 | DDC 385.09716/225—dc23

Nimbus Publishing acknowledges the financial support for its publishing activities from the Government of Canada, the Canada Council for the Arts, and from the Province of Nova Scotia. We are pleased to work in partnership with the Province of Nova Scotia to develop and promote our creative industries for the benefit of all Nova Scotians.

An inspection of the present Ocean Terminals of Halifax is sufficient to prove that it is practically impossible to make it a successful port at the present site and on the present lines, to be suitable either for continued business, for industrial enterprise or for a modern railway terminal or ocean port.[1]

–Frederick W. Cowie
Chief Engineer, Montréal Harbour Commission, July 1, 1913

Table of Contents

MAIN CHARACTERS

Arthur C. Brown	Senior engineer building the docks
George S. Campbell	Shipowner; became president of the Bank of Nova Scotia, was active in civic affairs
Frank Cochrane	Minister of Railways and Canals, Government of Canada
Frederick Cowie	Chief engineer, Montréal Harbour Commission, project designer
Francis William Whitney (FWW) Doane	City engineer, Halifax
W. A. Duff	Assistant chief engineer for Canadian Government Railways (CGR), then chief engineer after James McGregor
Michael Dwyer	Merchant and president, Halifax Board of Trade
Frederick Gutelius	General manager of CGR; was located in Moncton
H. W. Johnston	Acting city engineer while FWW Doane was overseas
E. B. McCurdy	Member of Parliament for Shelburne and Queens; succeeded Michael Dwyer as president of the Board of Trade
James McGregor	Chief engineer and project manager for CGR
Hugh R. Silver	Championed building of the Lord Nelson Hotel
Henry Thornton	First president of Canadian National Railways (CNR); instrumental in getting the Hotel Nova Scotian built
Andrew Wheaton	Manager of the consortium building the rail cut
Alfred N. Whitman	Lawyer and alderman

MAP OF HOMES

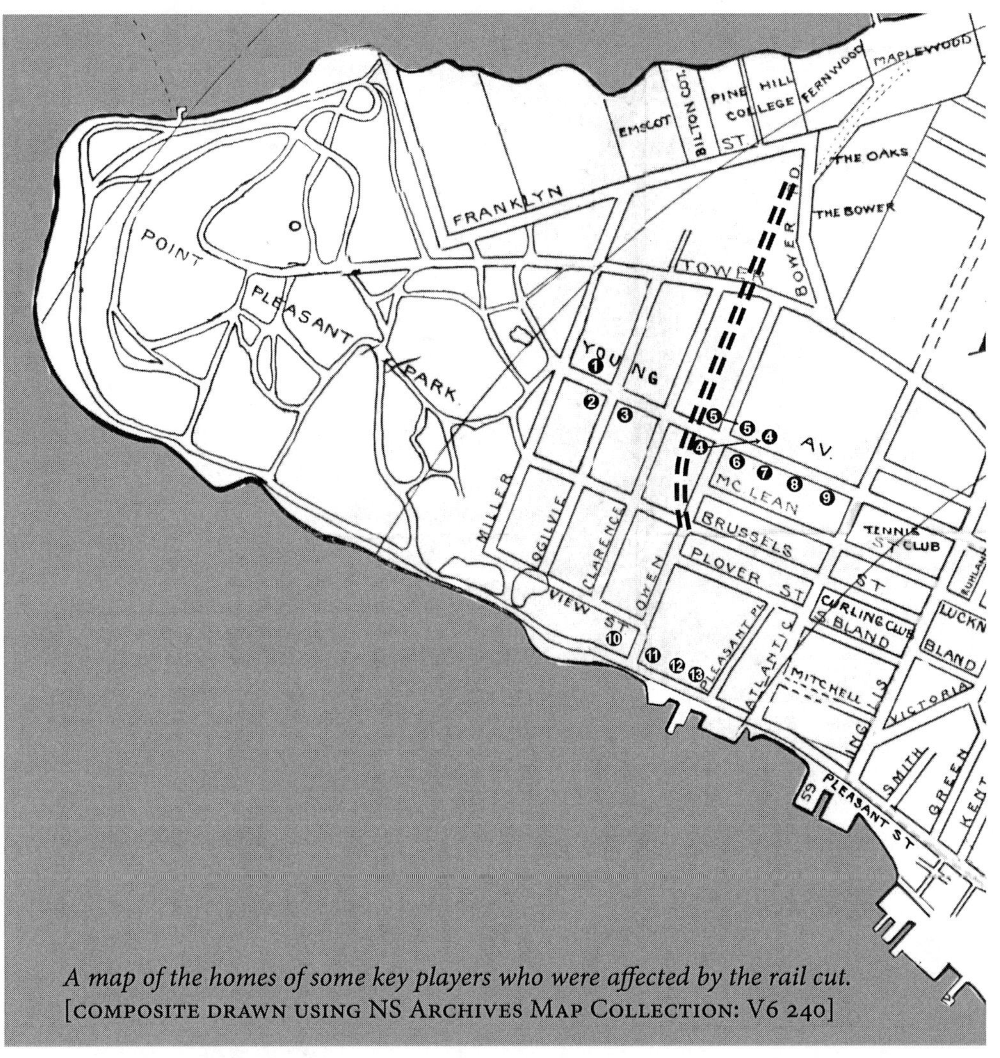

A map of the homes of some key players who were affected by the rail cut.
[COMPOSITE DRAWN USING NS ARCHIVES MAP COLLECTION: V6 240]

1. Alfred Whitman
2. Michael Dwyer
3. FWW Doane
4. C. Ochiltree Macdonald
5. Louisa Martin Smith (Pine Grove)
6. John MacInnes
7. George S. Campbell
8. W. A. Black
9. John Brookfield
10. Samuel Brookfield (Brookhurst)
11. Hugh Silver
12. Mrs. H. G. Bauld
13. Ella (Bauld) Oland

TIMELINE

Month	Year	Event
	1749	Halifax waterfront development begun
	1759	HM (British Royal Navy) Dockyard opened
Dec.	1858	Nova Scotia Railway opened between Halifax and Truro; development of Richmond Terminals
May	1866	William D. O'Brien started Halifax City Railroad Company
June	1877	North Street Station opened
	1877–80	Construction of Deep Water Terminus
	1881	Immigration facility opened at Pier 2 at Deepwater
	1890	Immigration facility at Pier 2 upgraded
Feb.	1895	Deepwater fire
May	1895	Richmond fire
Feb.	1897	New immigration quarters at Pier 2
Jan.	1907	ICR built Willow Park maintenance facilities
Oct.	1912	Port and railways project announcement by Frank Cochrane
Jan.	1913	Nova Scotia Construction Company started work on new Pier 2
Jan.	1913	Contract for rail cut won by Cook and Wheaton
Mar.	1913	Rail cut route released
May	1913	Residents of Gas Lane ordered to vacate houses
July	1913	F. W. Cowie report released
Autumn	1913	Port and railways project begun
June	1914–15	Breakwater built

Autumn	1915	Immigration facility at new Pier 2 opened
June	1916	Construction of numerous rail bridges begun
Nov.	1916	First ship docked at piers
Dec.	1916	First pier built to its full length
Dec. 6	1917	Halifax Explosion
Dec.	1917	Twelve bridges completed
Dec.	1919	Railway cut and docks completed
	1921	Pier A completed, Pier A1 partially infilled
Feb.	1928	Standard Construction Company completed new buildings at Pier 21
Mar.	1928	First immigrants arrived at Pier 21
	1932–34	Pier B built
	1955–60	Pier A1 completed
	1968	Halterm container terminal begun
May	1971	Pier 21 immigration centre closed
	1982	Fairview Cove container terminal opened

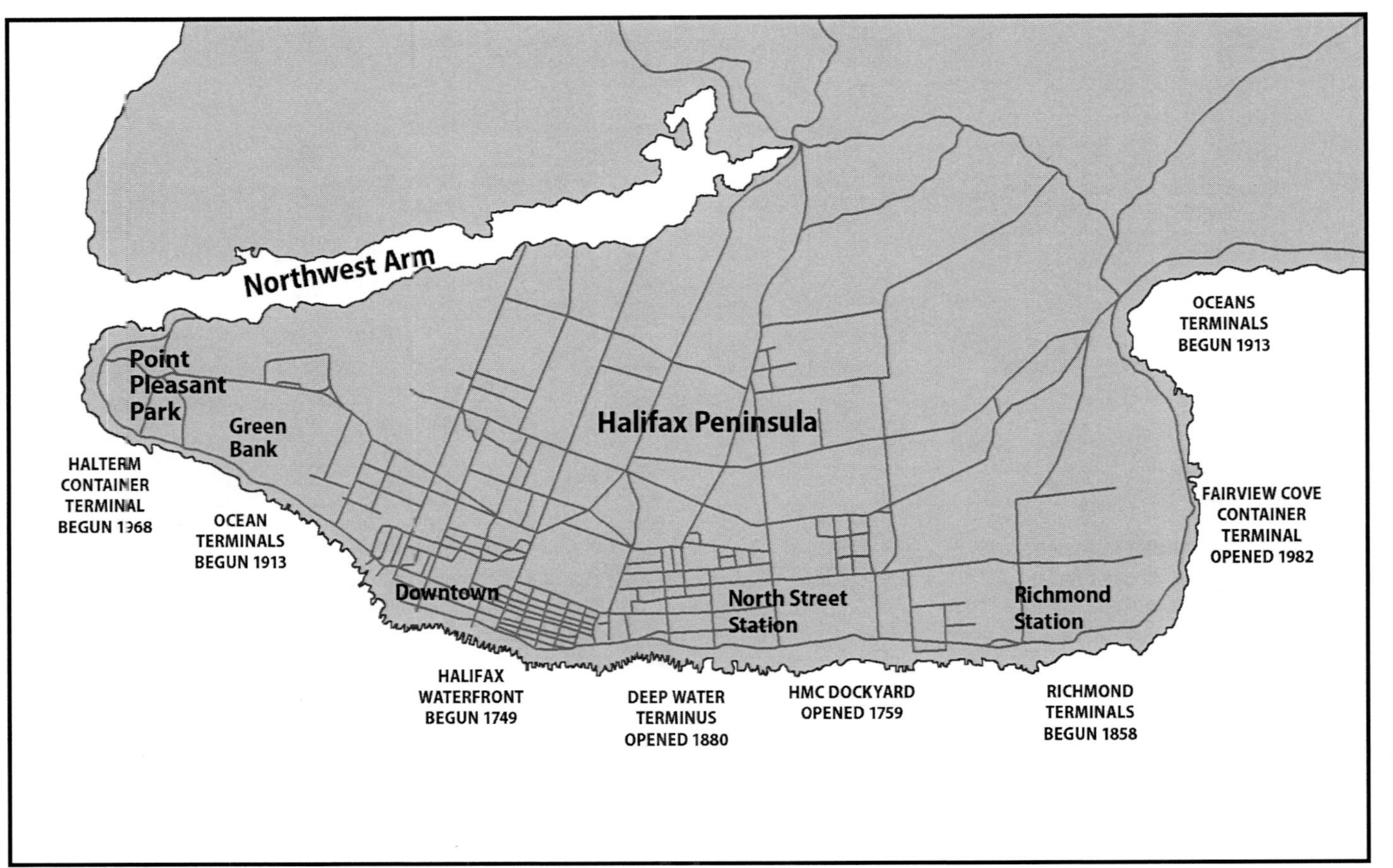

A timeline of key rail and port infrastructure development in Halifax.

INTRODUCTION

OUR LEGS CANNOT TAKE US FAR ON OUR BIG PLANET. FOR ALL BUT A TINY PART OF OUR TIME ON EARTH, virtually everybody died within sight of where they were born. Our ancestors were almost as immobile as the trees around them.

Perching atop a horse, mule, or camel, or sitting on a dog sled improved people's mobility, but these vehicles relied on the same energy sources as the rider: food, water, and rest. Only a conveyance that floated could take them any distance, but ships and boats also had a big limitation—they were of little use on the prairies of North America or in the deserts of Africa.

While figuring out a better way to pump water from mines, some smart people on the island of Great Britain perfected the steam engine. Boiling water under pressure until it was bursting to get out (the way some people felt about where they were born) released an enormous amount of energy that changed the world. It freed us to travel.

England's Stockton and Darlington Railway opened in 1825, towed by George Stephenson's Locomotion No. 1 steam engine. Great ribbons of land were set aside on which trees were felled, stones and gravel dumped, bridges built, and mountains blasted to make room for the trains. A railway network came into being and people and goods were on the move. Then in 1886 Karl Benz patented the automobile. Roads and highways were built for the automobile, gobbling up farmland and forest.

Fast, efficient long-distance mobility has been both the most valuable and the costliest of the benefits of the Industrial Revolution. The high point was the automobile. It became the driver of the world's economy, giving us a standard of living our ancestors never imagined. There has been no limit to the energy, ingenuity, oil, steel, and asphalt we will expend to feed our obsession with moving around.

Now, after just two hundred years, our planet is suffering. Our drive for mobility has ravaged the Earth and pushed us against the wall while we desperately look for a way to save the planet—while keeping our cars. We are in denial, not even broaching the obvious answer of limiting ourselves to electric buses, trains, ships, and perhaps even airplanes. From a curiosity to a convenience, cars have become a precious possession, a must for leisure and work, a release from boredom, a status symbol, a cultural spectacle—far too important to part with.

This all started with the train, when it showed us the possibilities. In a corner of eastern North America, at a time when cars were a novelty and the railway was king, a small city named Halifax was having mobility issues and was desperate for a fix.

CHAPTER 1

AN EXCITING DAY AT THE HALIFAX

The town of Halifax by no means impresses the visitor on his first entrance. The road from the station passes through some of the poorest thoroughfares and meanest houses.[2]

– Frederick W. Cowie, Chief Engineer,
Montréal Harbour Commission

July 1, 1913

IT WAS GOING TO BE A BIG DAY FOR MICHAEL DWYER—THE END OF A LONG, HARD STRUGGLE WITH THE federal government and the Intercolonial Railway. When he became president of the Halifax Board of Trade, with its six hundred members and twenty committees on everything from the West Indies to harbour pilot fees, he knew he had a big job ahead, but now, with only two months left in his term, he felt he had achieved his goal.

He counted the chimes from the clock in the parlour. One…two… three…four…five. There was no going back to sleep, so he got up in the dark, ate a leisurely breakfast, put on his best suit, and stepped outside into the crisp morning air. It was October 30, 1912. He would break with his routine and walk to the office at the venerable Halifax wholesaling firm of John Tobin & Co. He had inherited the business from his father, also named Michael, when he was just twenty-five. Now he was thirty-seven and comfortably situated. He was optimistic that today's events would open the door to even greater prosperity for the family business that his father had inherited from Great-Uncle John himself.

Being comfortably situated meant he could afford to live on Young Avenue, the most exclusive street in the city, protected by a provincial law restricting development to private, architect-designed residences that cost at least $5,000 to construct and were set back no less than twelve metres from the street. Before construction could even begin, plans had to be approved by the city engineer, Francis William Whitney Doane, known to all as "FWW." When Michael wanted to build a stable on his property, FWW approved the request. It was what good neighbours did.

> In round figures a 1912 dollar equates to $33 in 2025. In 1917, the highest paid person on city staff, the city engineer, was paid $3,000. The typical annual income for a janitor had just been raised to $700. With the coming of Prohibition, the Nova Scotia Temperance Alliance recommended a salary of $1,800 for the Liquor Inspector. City Council decided to pay him $1,500 per annum.

As he walked past FWW's house in the muted morning light, Michael Dwyer reflected on how today's announcement would affect the powerful city engineer. His life would certainly become complicated. C. Ochiltree Macdonald, who lived in the next house, would probably have to move, as would Louisa Smith, his neighbour. But he would not have to move.

Move from Young Avenue? No, definitely not, he reassured himself.

Getting to this day had certainly been a trial. At the beginning of 1911, when he had become president, the biggest issue facing the board—as usual—was the sad state of the port facilities: terminals and sheds jammed into neighbourhoods; people having to dodge moving trains to get to work; wagons, automobiles, and locomotives sharing the same thoroughfares; a mishmash of sun-bleached worm-eaten wooden wharves; inadequate immigration facilities; railroad infrastructure spread all over the city instead of neatly packed into one place. Halifax was the closest mainland North American port to Europe. Confederation had come forty-five years earlier. That had been more than enough time to make Halifax Canada's main port of entry and a bustling hub of activity—profitable activity—but the rail and shipping services to the city were not making the grade.

It was not the board's fault. Their efforts had convinced Sir Wilfrid Laurier's federal government to commission a study, and John Kennedy, an engineer with the Port of Montréal, had arrived in August 1910. Kennedy's report had come in May 1911, recommending four new 244-metre docks. On June 1, *The Morning Chronicle* had reported that a tender was forthcoming; Parliament had already appropriated the money. Board of Trade members were thrilled. But their president was not. Michael Dwyer had considered it a stopgap. If they were finally going to turn Halifax into a world-class port for Canada, they needed to do it right, once and for all.

To halt the momentum, Dwyer had known that nothing less than an assault on the federal government could save the day. He had arrived in Ottawa the morning of May 2, 1911, leading a delegation that included the mayor and a councillor, seven Board of Trade delegates including himself, six representatives of shipping companies—two from the Intercolonial Railway—and one other. They met with Prime Minister Laurier and three cabinet ministers, along with two MPs from Halifax: A. B. Crosby and Robert Borden. They spent two days and walked away with a commitment for badly needed improvements to the four existing docks of the Deep Water Terminus located in the harbour just south of HMC Dockyard, which had a new occupant: the brand new Royal Canadian Navy.

Three months later, the government contracted the Nova Scotia Construction Company to build a much larger replacement for Deep Water Terminus Pier 2, with a budget of $1.5 million. That was all that would materialize from Kennedy's report—because Michael Dwyer and his entourage had planted a seed for something greater.

Robert L. Borden, the leader of the opposition, had listened carefully to the presentations over those two days. Five months later, on October 10, 1911, his Conservatives came into power with a new, expanded vision for Canadian trade. The Port of Halifax figured prominently in that vision. Even though Michael Dwyer was a Liberal, for once in his life he didn't mind having a Conservative prime minister in Ottawa. That was because he knew the new PM personally. Robert Borden represented the riding of Halifax.

Expectations were high now, on October 30, 1912, because the man who would implement Borden's vision was in town. The minister of Railways and Canals, Frank Cochrane, had been working on it throughout the past year. He had appointed Frederick Cowie, chief engineer of the Montréal Harbour Commission, and a staff of engineers to undertake an exhaustive examination of what was needed to move the Port of Halifax into the big leagues.

Now Cowie's report was ready for prime time. The tables were being set for today's luncheon at the Halifax Hotel—"The Halifax," as it was known. Three hundred Board of Trade members were donning their best togs. The word on the street was that Cochrane would make a big announcement about ship and rail service to Halifax.

Michael Dwyer's big day was dawning.

CHAPTER 2

RICHMOND RAILWAYS AND DEEPWATER DOCKS

If it only wakes the people up it does some good. And more, it inspires them with hope and confidence that things will yet go on successfully, and that Halifax will outlive the opprobrium with which she is frequently assailed. The Rail Road will be accomplished if the people will but act in unity and harmony. The time for croaking is past.[3]

–Editorial, *Halifax Morning Journal*, June 23, 1854

THE OLDEST AND CHEAPEST WAY TO MOVE GOODS AND PEOPLE IS ON THE OCEAN. AFTER SHIPS, HARBOURS are key to that system. The world has many big harbours, but big harbours are not necessarily good harbours. In the early days of shipping, all that mattered was that a harbour provided shelter from storms, pirates, and enemy navies. If it was big and sheltered, it was considered a good harbour. But if not cared for, good harbours silt up, navigational aids deteriorate, worms weaken the docks. There are lots of ways they can become poor harbours.

Halifax is not just a good harbour; it's a great harbour. It's sheltered and, yes, it's big, but it has other vital features. Many harbours have rivers flowing into them, carrying millions of tons of silt that has to be constantly dredged to keep today's increasingly larger ships from striking bottom. That is not a problem for Halifax. There is no river of consequence, and the water is deep, even close to shore. Some harbours don't have good anchorage. An early commentator noted that Halifax could hold all the ships of Britain's Royal Navy, the world's largest, in safety where they would not be in one another's way. Some harbours

Halifax's deep harbour and numerous piers can easily accommodate massive cruise ships like the Queen Mary 2, *shown here sailing remarkably close to shore in Halifax in 2004.* [AUTHOR PHOTO]

freeze over in winter. Not Halifax. In some harbours it's difficult to build docks because the land is low and hard to approach. Almost all of the one hundred kilometres of shoreline inside Halifax Harbour can easily be docked.

Even though Royal Navy planners like the famous Captain James Cook immediately appreciated Halifax Harbour's potential as a naval port, the effort to make it a successful commercial port has been another matter. It had always been busy, but on the day Michael Dwyer walked downtown it was not handling anywhere near the business it could and should have been. Since the founding of the town in 1749, the port had existed for the Royal Navy, but those days were over. The Royal Navy had sailed away in 1907.

Halifax had a problem. It was in the wrong place in thinly populated Canada. The route to Canada's heartland was the St. Lawrence River, which carried ships directly to the population centres like Quebec and Montréal and on into Ontario. Halifax was away from the action, stuck in a sparsely populated area out on the shores of the Atlantic Ocean—perfect for a naval base, but isolated from the country's builders, spenders, movers, and shakers.

Railways brought hope. A railway could make Halifax the winter mail port for British North America. In summer, the all-important mail bound from Europe to the colonies left the Atlantic Ocean before getting anywhere close to Halifax and went up the St. Lawrence River in ships of the Montreal Ocean Steamship Company—the Allan Line—toward the key Canadian population centres, but with the coming of winter the St. Lawrence froze and was closed to shipping. When that happened, the mail went through an American port. The mail ships breezed past ice-free Halifax and tied up at Portland, Maine. There, passengers and mail got on the train to Montréal, the biggest city and the financial centre of Canada.

It seemed to make sense. The train ride was less than one-third the distance a train from Halifax would take. But it took the ships longer to get to Portland from Europe as they sailed close to, but past Halifax to connect with a Portland train. Halifax needed a railway connection. That way, the mail could be unloaded from the slow-moving ships and onto the faster trains sooner and, even though the rail distance was farther, the mail would get to Montréal faster than if it had gone by slow boat to Portland.

⌗⌗⌗⌗⌗⌗⌗⌗

On September 19, 1839, Nova Scotia's first railway had begun hauling coal six miles alongside the East River in Pictou County. Three steam locomotives replaced the hundred or so horses they had been using to haul carloads of coal on tracks from the Albion Mine in Stellarton, NS, to the pier there. Premier Joseph Howe became an enthusiastic railway advocate. On November 29, 1851, his government passed an act with the ambitious plan to "make provision for the construction of a Trunk Railway through British North America."[4] The initial goals were modest, with just two routes. One would go from Halifax to Windsor, on the Bay of Fundy, to connect with shipping to Saint John and the United States. The second would go to Truro, with plans to eventually continue to Pictou and connect shipping with Prince Edward Island and the St. Lawrence River.

They turned the sod on June 13, 1854, and got to work the next day.[5] The first engine, the *Mayflower*, fuelled by wood, not coal, arrived in January 1855, and the next month it was running trials on the six kilometres of track that had been laid. They kept building and reached Windsor on June 3, 1858, and Truro on December 15, 1858. Two daily trains ran to and from Truro. The trip took four hours because of the moderate speed and the ten stops, the first of which was between Halifax and Bedford. Today Truro to Halifax takes an hour to drive, but four hours was spectacular compared with the stagecoach.

It was a historic achievement that would change Nova Scotia as it was changing the world. Large-scale movement of goods, people, and mail had always been possible aboard ships on the seas, rivers, and canals, but not on land. Railways changed that. The rise of national brands is just one example of how railways changed everything. Before refrigeration, when vegetables had to last up to a year, vast quantities of pickles and relish were made in every city, town, and hamlet, and they were consumed not as a garnish on hot dogs but as a main course. It was a given that they were eaten where they were made—unless they could be put on a ship and sold in another seaport. It was way too expensive to move them overland, so virtually everything used in landlocked communities was produced locally. Rail opened up the continent, enabling American Henry Heinz to sell his pickles everywhere.

But it took more than just trains and tracks. It took storage. To be a big player, a seaport needed vast areas to hold boxes, crates, and barrels of goods arriving by sea and waiting for a train, and vice versa. Big, dry, secure sheds had to be built on flat areas nearby. Halifax could easily handle the ships but finding all the space—not only for goods but for fuel, maintenance facilities, rail yards, a passenger station, and hotels—was a big headache that could scuttle the whole dream. Increasingly large quantities of goods, people, and mail were arriving by ship from Europe. All had to be unloaded, temporarily stored, protected from thieves, organized by destination, and loaded aboard not just any train but the right train. The best place for storage was a shed right on the dock, minimizing the distance from ship to train, and therefore cost.

The first track in 1858 had been built from Richmond, where land was cheap, and ran north along the Bedford Basin toward Windsor Junction, where it divided toward Windsor and Truro. Today, Richmond is part of Halifax, but then it was five kilometres away, close to where the MacKay Bridge crosses the harbour. A way into the city was needed, where the people were, but it wasn't easy. The route was straight and flat but narrow and full of impediments. A lot of expensive waterfront land would have to be acquired, and money was scarce. The first obstruction was the Royal Navy Dockyard, the reason Halifax was settled in 1749. Britannia ruled the waves in the western Atlantic because the dockyard was in Halifax. Then came the waterfront, the domain of well-entrenched companies like the Cunard shipping line and other shipowners, along with powerful organizations like the Royal Engineers and Her Majesty's Ordnance Yard. Threading the tracks through these obstacles required time, money, and patience. It would have to wait. At least they had finished the railway.

At the foot of Vestry and Duffus Streets, where the tracks began in Richmond, the infrastructure for the Halifax depot was erected, with a roundhouse for turning engines around, a passenger station, repair shops, and freight sheds.[6] Shoreline was available for two docks to enable ships and railway cars to meet, ensuring a smooth movement of goods. More would come later.

To get from the station to the city, passengers had to walk or take a horse-drawn conveyance. After eight years of muddy roads, frozen ruts, snow, and ice, the taxi service improved moderately in May of 1866 when "a shrewd little man named O'Brien"[7]—William O'Brien—opened his Halifax City Railroad Company. With this service, two horses towed a "horse car" on railway tracks. The weather was the same, but the car had a roof, the ride was smoother, and the price was better. The service ran from the Richmond Station through downtown to Inglis Street.

> Those docks at the Richmond Terminals have since been rebuilt, expanded, and upgraded several times and still exist today, handling specialized cargoes that other terminals are unable to accommodate.

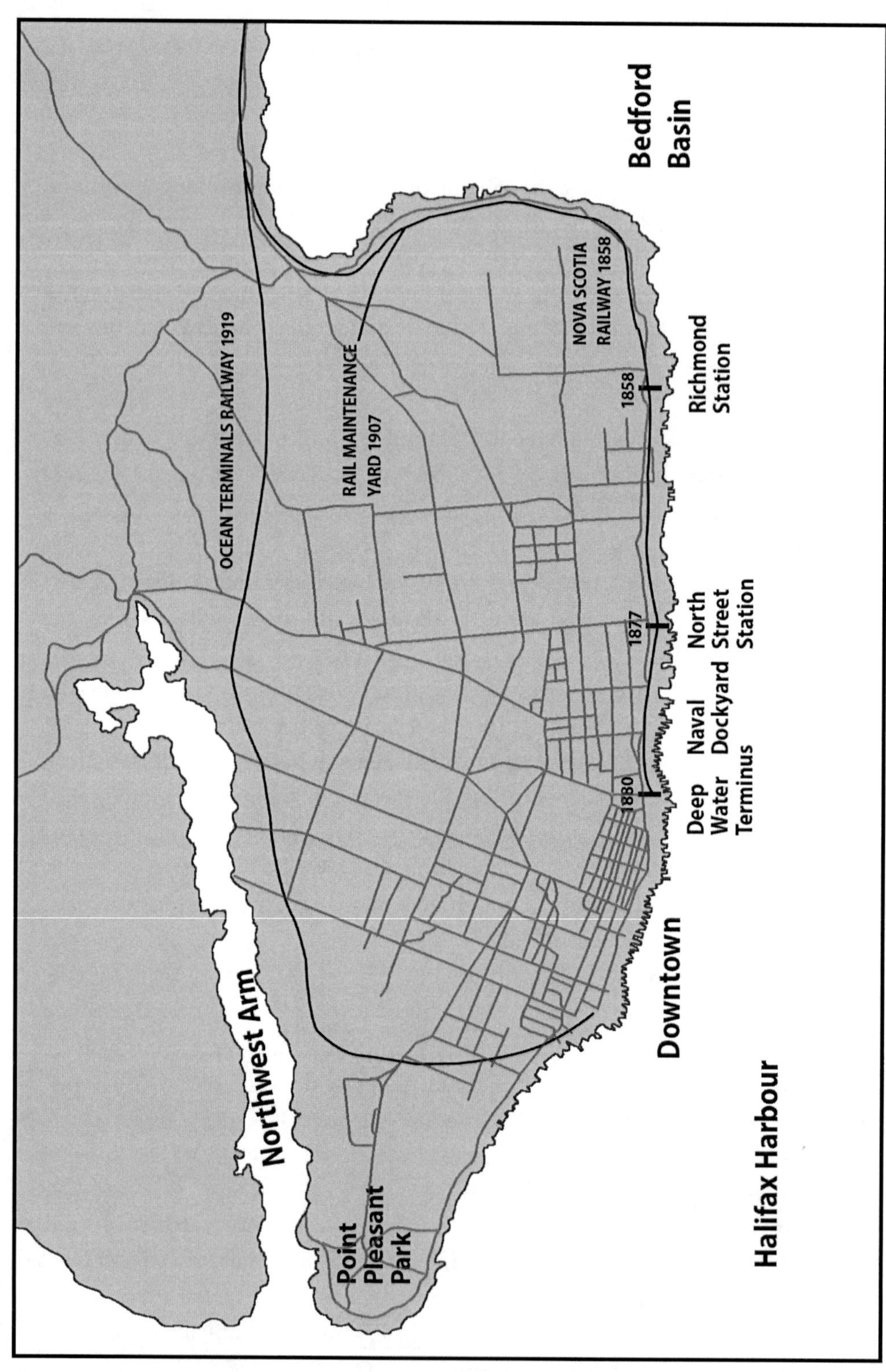

A map of the Halifax peninsula showing early rail and shipping infrastructure.
[AUTHOR SKETCH]

Looking north toward the Bedford Basin, ca. early 1900s. Note the wall separating the boxcars from the houses. The first passenger station was north of the sugar refinery, the tall building in the distance. [NS ARCHIVES, N-7014]

The passenger service was inconvenient but, in the shipment of freight, Richmond became unworkable as the freight business grew. In the fall of 1871, the Halifax Chamber of Commerce passed a resolution favouring a new terminus near the waterfront in the centre of the city.

The Royal Navy blocked it. The railway builders had planned a route through the naval dockyard because the Admiralty in London had told Joseph Howe they could—then they changed their minds.

Everybody had had enough of Richmond. A study in 1873 suggested a line terminating on the South Common not far from the Public Gardens. Another advocated a terminus in Dartmouth. In desperation, federal engineers came up with a way to squeeze the tracks outside the dockyard wall along the east side of Upper Water Street. It would be tight, with the dockyard on one side and steep hills on the other, and with no room for freight sheds. In 1874, the Dominion government suggested that the freight and passenger traffic could be separated, with a new passenger station closer to Halifax while the freight depot would continue to be at Richmond, with steamboats shuttling cargo to and from downtown—a kluge if there ever was one!

An 1875 report prepared by City Council noted that the expense of moving goods from the city to the train was often as great as the cost of transportation to the final destination. Twenty percent of the transportation cost for freight from England was for the trip from the train to the consignee in Halifax, and it was 50 percent of the transportation cost to and from some points in the United States.[8]

Confederation had brought money and improvements. The carrot that had lured Nova Scotia into becoming a charter member of the four-province federation was the promise of a railway between Halifax and Canada's interior.

Railway engineer Sandford Fleming began work on the route between Truro and the terminus of the Grand Trunk Railway at Rivière-du-Loup, Quebec. That vital piece of track opened in 1876, with the first train from Halifax (likely carrying both passengers and freight) arriving at Quebec on July 4. It signified the birth of the Intercolonial Railway (ICR), one of the great early railways of Canada, along with the Grand Trunk, the Canadian Northern, and, of course, the Canadian Pacific Railways.

For Halifax, the ICR would bring two benefits. The first, the connection with Montréal, was obvious. The second was the opportunity to move the terminus into the city.

On January 19, 1875, City Council, facing pressure from Ottawa, appointed a committee of aldermen (as city councillors were then known) to identify a site for a station closer to the downtown. They sent three delegates to the capital with yet another proposal. More failure. Two weeks later, the feds took over and issued a tender for construction of a new station on a piece of land they had managed to scrounge near where the Macdonald Bridge comes ashore today.

\+\+\+\+\+\+\+\+\+\+\+\+\+\+

Architect and builder Henry Peters delivered—two months early—what some would call the finest railway station in the Dominion. At 5:00 P.M. on August 8, 1877, Prime Minister Alexander Mackenzie arrived on the first passenger train. The next day, the North Street Station was officially opened, serving the ICR and Windsor and Annapolis Railways.

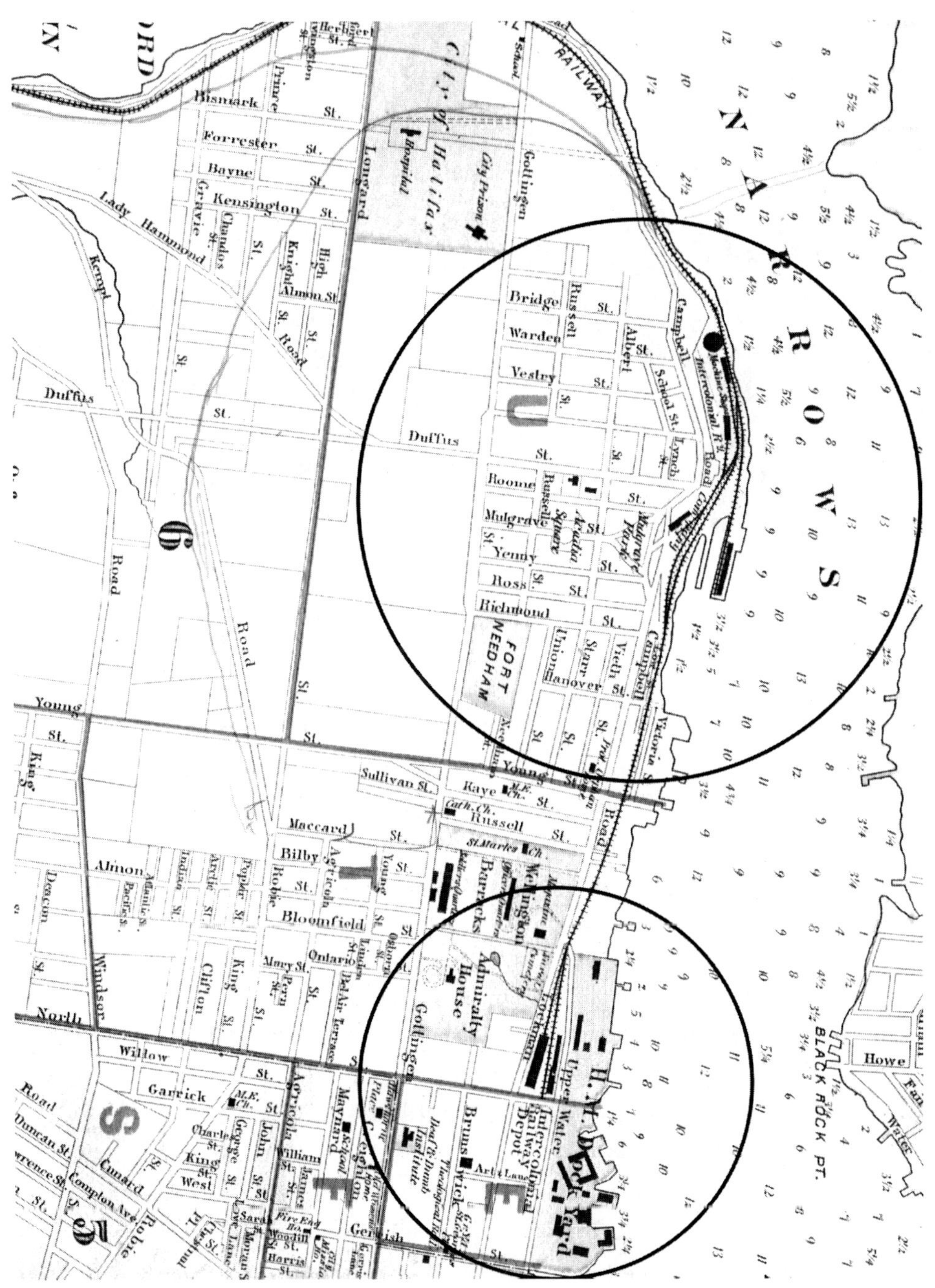

A portion of an 1878 map showing the location of the Richmond Terminals (circled area at top) and the naval dockyard (circled area at bottom).
[H. W. Hopkins NS Archives Library O/S G 1129 H3 H67 1878]

The North Street Station was on the side of a hill. Note the stone wall on the left of the image, which supports Lockman Street, which became Barrington Street. There is a rail car below the wall on the right. [Notman Studio NS Archives 1983-310 number 100056]

The station was a far cry from the bare-bones structure it replaced. An imposing edifice 35 metres wide, built of uniform pressed brick on a granite base, it had three storeys with towers at the four corners and a high central clock tower 21 metres above the ground. One of the most striking buildings in the city, with varnished floors and steam heating, it was the epitome of grace and function. It was lit by gas chandeliers that burned coal gas produced at the gas plant located where the new docks would be built. Two covered platforms 122 metres long enabled comfortable boarding of the trains. It would be Halifax's railway station for the next forty years—a fine building in an awkward spot.

Closer to town than the old one but still not where it needed to be, the North Street Station was cut into the side of the escarpment that runs along the whole of the peninsula, with a step down toward the rail yard and a step up to what today is Barrington Street.

The location of the splendid new North Street Station was problematic. Passengers arrived too far away from their destinations and were still obliged to use the horse train to get to where people lived. But during construction, after a set-to with the ICR over the use of his rails,

William O'Brien, who was probably not making the money he had expected with his street railway, had decided to get out of the business. He auctioned off his fifty horses and equipment, and over the next twenty years four more companies had a go at running a horse railway service between downtown Halifax and the North Street Station.

In the spring of 1896, the last horse-drawn car made its final trip. The Halifax Electric Tramway Company had brought electric streetcars to Halifax. That company would eventually become the Nova Scotia Light and Power company and eventually Nova Scotia Power. Michael Dwyer's father was a major investor, as was Henry M. Whitney, the driving force behind the steel plant in Sydney, Nova Scotia.

The railway presence in Richmond encouraged industry to develop and soon Halifax builders like Samuel Brookfield had established a sugar refinery, a textile mill, a dry dock, and other enterprises in the area.

The first bridge across Halifax Harbour went up in 1884, a railway bridge just under half a kilometre long with supports reaching down twenty to twenty-five metres and a swing bridge to let ships into the basin. The first train crossed in March 1885; daily passenger service began in January 1886 from Dartmouth's new station near Park Avenue, where CN Rail keeps engines today.

Unfortunately, the bridge didn't last long. On December 7, 1891, a hurricane destroyed it. It was rebuilt. That one floated away on a high tide in the early hours of July 23, 1893. The harbour was no place for a wooden railway bridge.

Dartmouth's business and political leaders decided they had had enough of bridges and pressed the federal government for their own rail line to Windsor Junction, where the original Nova Scotia Railway split between Windsor and Truro. In January 1896 work began on that link.[9]

To alleviate the inconvenience and expense of shipping freight through Richmond, the federal government acquired shoreline closer to the city—near where the casino is today—and in June 1877 James

Kennedy and Co. began construction of new piers and sheds sufficient to handle twelve ships.

They built a set of four docks, Piers 2 through 5, which would eventually grow to five docks. Called the Deep Water Terminus, or just "Deepwater," the docks jutted out into the harbour to supplement piers 6 through 9 at the Richmond Terminals. These were sizeable wharves up to 213 metres long and able to handle the biggest steamships of the day. At the original Pier 2, basic facilities were set up to process immigrants to Canada. There was even a tall grain elevator, opened in 1882, a sign of Canada's growing status as a wheat exporter.

By 1912 the Deep Water Terminus was showing its age. Frederick Cowie, architect of the new vision, observed in his *Report to the Honourable Frank Cochrane on Halifax Harbour*: "Visitors to Halifax who remain to learn of its wonderful attractions...adversely criticize the first views and impressions gained of it from the old wooden landing quays with their lack of facilities for steamships, the railway station, and the thoroughfares leading to the city."[10]

Deepwater also suffered from the same problem that plagued Richmond—a lack of space to expand, being cramped on one side by the dockyard and on the other side by the city, and the steep grade. Railways at the end of the line, like Halifax, need lots of tracks on which to store and sort cars as they configure new trains, and if they want to expand the freight traffic, they need increasingly bigger storage sheds. It all takes space. By the turn of the century, it was well known that more had to be developed if Halifax were to meet its potential as a world-class commercial port.

The pressure had been mounting. In 1904 and again in 1906, Frederick Cowie had accompanied the minister of Marine and Fisheries on an inspection of the harbour, trying to come up with a site that would overcome the inadequacies once and for all. In January 1907, ICR officials were forced to build new maintenance shops and a roundhouse to replace the old and inadequate facilities at Richmond. They evaluated five sites nearby, but all were unsuitable, and ended up in a large area at Windsor and Young Streets, far away from Richmond. A double track, called the Willow Park Branch, ran from the Richmond Yards in a wide circle across Lady Hammond Road and Kempt Road

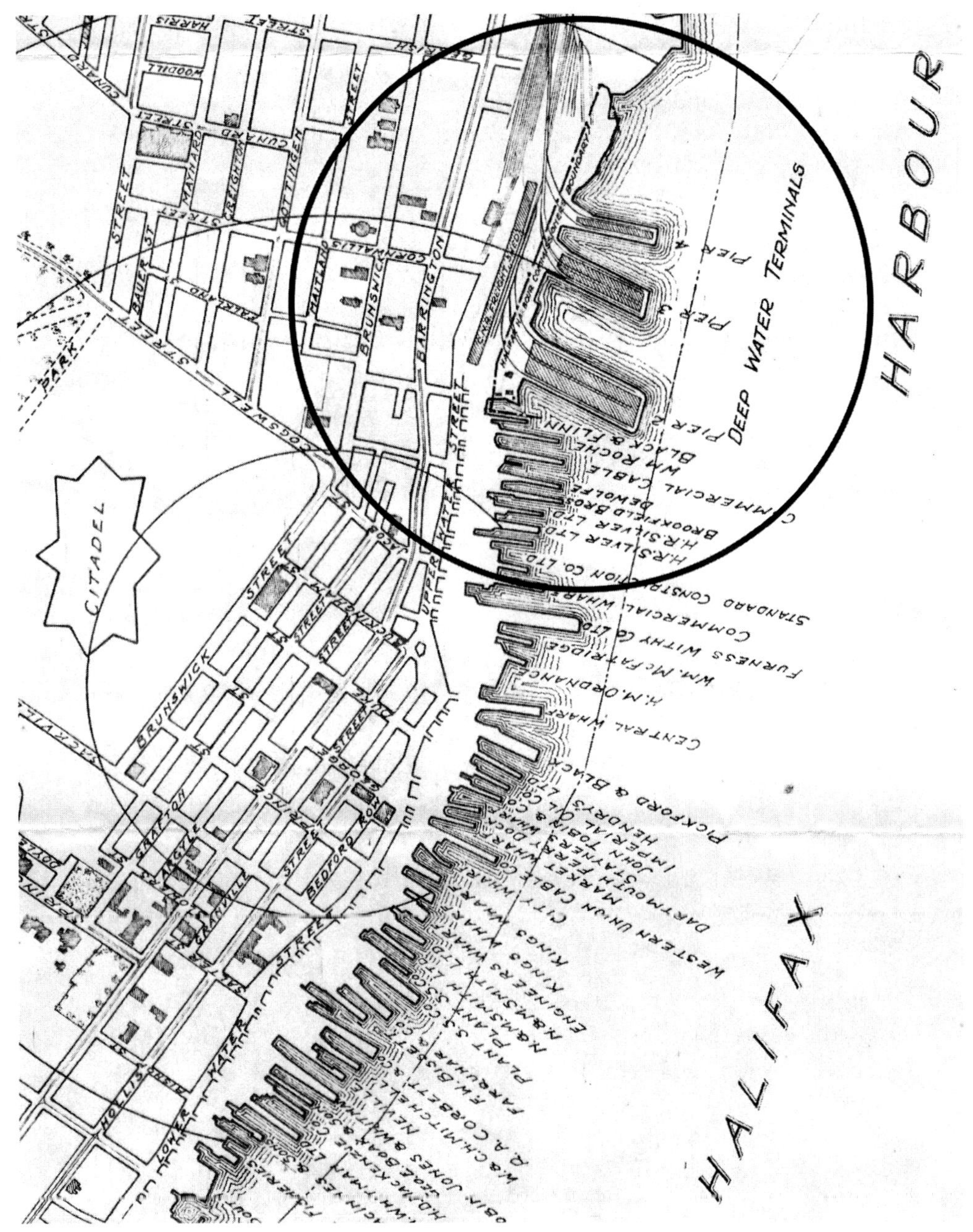

A portion of a 1930 Halifax map depicting the location of the Deep Water Terminus (circled). The large Furness Withy Company wharf just below the circle is today called Purdy's Wharf. [Halifax Municipal Archives CR10-087]

to the Willow Park Yard, as it was called. (Some of the railway bridges are still there.) Meanwhile, the tenacious Board of Trade, supported by almost all of the twenty or so dock owners, was pressuring the railway to extend service from Deepwater to the Halifax waterfront in the downtown area. They even presented the railway with a design.

++++++++++++++++

In 1896, when Halifax lawyer Robert Borden had been elected to the House of Commons in the riding of Halifax, he'd campaigned on a platform of making Halifax the Atlantic winter port for Canada. On October 10, 1911, he became the prime minister and in November, he was in Halifax introducing his minister of Railways and Canals, Frank Cochrane.

In May 1912, Cochrane was back, inspecting transportation infrastructure and meeting with Michael Dwyer and other expectant business leaders, but he was maddeningly uncommunicative. The luncheons, dinners, and offline conversations had a common theme, summed up by his Conservative colleague, F. B. McCurdy, the newly elected MP for Shelburne and Queens and soon to succeed Michael Dwyer as president of the Board of Trade: Make Halifax the Atlantic gateway for the Dominion.

Now, five months later, Cochrane was back for the big reveal. The group assembling at The Halifax to hear him on October 30, 1912, hoped the big day had finally arrived. These were men with the most to gain from an expansion of port facilities at Halifax. When the minister took the podium, they were bursting with anticipation. Before long, they were on their feet. Not only was it better than they expected—it far exceeded anything they had hoped for.

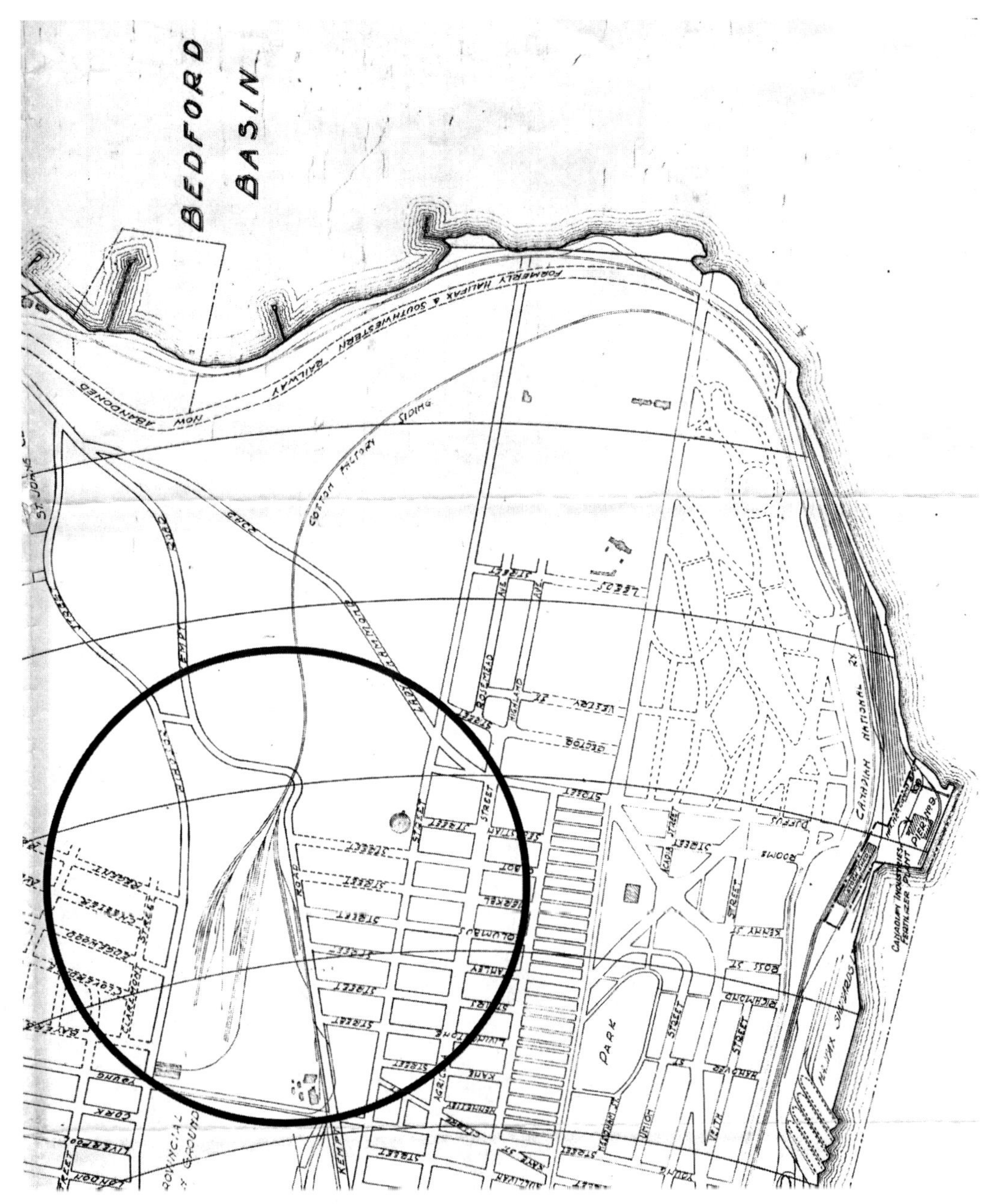

This section of a 1930 Halifax map depicts the location of the Willow Park Rail Maintenance Yard at Young and Windsor Streets (circled).
[Halifax Municipal Archives CR10-087]

CHAPTER 3

FOR HE'S A JOLLY GOOD FELLOW

This is the greatest thing for Halifax that has ever been put forward—there can be no doubt of that.[11]

– Andrew M. Bell, Halifax Merchant

THE APPLAUSE WAS LONG AND LOUD AS COCHRANE ENTERED THE DINING ROOM. JOINING HIM AT THE HEAD table were local members of parliament and members of the legislature, who got themselves invited, along with prominent businessmen—all with a keen interest. They included hardware merchant Andrew M. Bell, William A. Black of shipowners Pickford & Black, and shipowner George S. Campbell. His docks were the last to operate a marine business on the original Halifax waterfront. They were demolished in 2020 to make space for the boardwalk, along which hundreds of thousands of tourists now walk every summer. From that site the harbour tugs, including the boats of Campbell's Halifax Tow Boat Company, came and went for a century and a half.

Michael Dwyer did not disappoint his eager colleagues as he welcomed Cochrane, thanking him for his efforts on behalf of the Port of Halifax. Then, it came. Three hundred breaths were drawn in and held as Cochrane took the podium. He immediately pronounced that he understood what they had been living through and declared that his plan was not only for the city but for the whole Dominion of Canada. Over the past year his government had had the best experts available working on the solution. Then he announced two aspects to the project.

First, the docks:

> These are to extend for one and a half miles from the Lumber Yard to Point Pleasant Park and will consist of six piers 1,250 feet long and 800 feet in width with capacity sufficient to dock at least thirty ships. There will be one bulk head loading pier 2,000 feet in length, at which the ocean greyhounds will land. This pier will be equipped with immigration buildings, sheds and a grain elevator.

In other words, a whole new waterfront was planned, south of the existing one. Then, the trains:

> A new union passenger station will be erected at the end of Hollis Street, which will be of ample size and suitable architecture.
>
> These terminals will be approached by a double-tracked railroad which will...extend southerly through the low divide between Bedford Basin and the head of the North West Arm. It will then skirt the Arm in such location as will do the least damage to property in that vicinity, avoiding all level crossings and, for the most part, passing through deep cuttings, so as not to mar the beauty of that district, and finally reaching the terminals by passing under the lower end of Young Avenue. The streets in the residential district, where the railway is submerged, will be carried over the cuttings on artistic bridges in keeping with the present surroundings. At the terminal ample tracks will be provided for the economical handling of the business for the wharves and union station; also, proper facilities for the housing of engines and the care of passenger cars.

The audience was ecstatic, unable to believe what they were hearing. As *The Halifax Herald* reported,

> The scene was thrilling when the minister of railways rose. Cheers rang out, handkerchiefs waved and there were signs of intense rejoicing as he made his announcement, so fraught with vital interest to those who heard it. Every word was listened to almost

> with baited [*sic*] breath, and on the conclusion the company again came to its feet, cheers rang out, handkerchiefs fluttered and "He's a Jolly Good Fellow" was sung with enthusiastic gusto.[12]

Cochrane presented the plan to sink the railbed into the earth as a measure to minimize inconvenience to Haligonians, but it was equally to reduce the grade. Trains don't do well on hills and the Halifax peninsula is a plateau roughly forty to fifty metres above sea level. The engineers had to get the tracks as close to sea level as possible.

If it were to cost $35 million ($1.155 billion in today's money)—which was the amount on everybody's lips, even though Cochrane had not discussed the outlay—it would be the biggest public works project in the city's history. Over time, this massive upgrade to rail and port infrastructure would become known as the Ocean Terminals, but it was destined not to unfold as expected. World War I was around the corner, followed by the Halifax Explosion. It would actually turn into a series of projects that would change the geography of Halifax and continue off and on for more than a century.

Halifax was a city of only forty-five thousand people. What caused a problem so big it required this kind of money to fix—the equivalent of $26,000 for every person?

‡‡‡‡‡‡‡‡‡‡‡‡‡‡‡‡

The problem was geography—not the harbour but the land. Ironically, in this part of big, empty Canada there was a lack of space. Eons of time had carved a complicated shoreline into Halifax Harbour.

Much of Halifax is a huge peninsula that juts into the middle of this harbour, a peninsula that glaciers and time have so eroded as to make it almost an island. If the peninsula were removed, Halifax Harbour would no longer be a harbour. It would be a bay, and the city would have grown up on the shores of the bay, in the same way that Toronto has grown up on the shores of Lake Ontario, with lots of room to expand around at least half its circumference. In 1749, the city fathers chose this peninsula for their town because they wanted to live inside this magnificent, sheltered harbour. It was an ideal location with a crucial advantage; it was tricky to sail into, which made it easy to defend at a time when defence was vital.

But things change, and the geography that made it so attractive in 1749 made it challenging in 1912. By that time, the city had not yet grown to occupy the whole peninsula, but it soon would; today it has spilled onto what is called mainland Halifax (as opposed to "on the peninsula") and is sprawling at an alarming rate.

In the fifty years spent building and operating their creation the railway moguls had been unable to take the train to the people. If Halifax had been planted across the harbour where Dartmouth is, there would not have been a problem. There was plenty of room, but it was too late. Halifax was not going to move, so the south end of the city had to be changed. The challenge was to find a place that put the docks, the passenger station, the freight sheds, and the people in close proximity to one another, but not on top of one another, so society could get on with its most urgent aim—unlimited mobility to satisfy its unyielding desire to be somewhere else. All this had to be on the peninsula because that was where the people were, and the people were bursting to move around.

While he was the prime minister of the United Kingdom, the Duke of Wellington was asked what he thought of the new railways that were just getting built. He didn't think much of them, he declared, because "they will only cause the lower classes to move about needlessly."[13] Needlessly or not, they and all the other classes were determined to move around.

However, with what he was proposing, Frank Cochrane faced more than geographic obstacles. While the announcement was thrilling for Michael Dwyer and the Board of Trade, not everybody was a member of that exclusive and influential club. They saw danger ahead. The natural beauty of Halifax, which so many dearly loved, was under threat.

The reaction in the room to Cochrane's announcement indicated clearly that he had chosen the best venue in which to introduce the government's plans. He had barely planted his feet at the podium when he declared,

> I wish...to express my appreciation of the assistance which has been rendered by your Board of Trade and especially by my good friend Mr. Dwyer, the president who is in the chair. I am glad that this announcement is to be made at a purely business meeting. It is a business matter regarding which we can meet on common ground.[14]

What he was hearing was not new to Michael Dwyer. He and others had been kept in the loop—like a group of co-conspirators.[15]

The engineers Cochrane had retained to attack the problem had studied four locations and concluded that there was only one way to do it: The train had to be routed through the city, which entailed upheaval and a good deal of risk. There was no hope that it would not be controversial.

Even though the conservative *Herald* laid down its battle cry with the headline, "The Red Blood of Halifax Backs the Colossal New Scheme to the Very Last Man," not all, even all the people in the room, were yet on board. J. E. DeWolf of the steamship and mercantile firm T. A. S. DeWolf, a man with much to gain from the new project, noted, "The proposition is so big that we must have time to consider it ere we make any statement."[16] And coal merchant Senator William Roche added cautiously, "I must have time to consider the proposition.... The scheme proposes such a radical departure from present conditions that I am fairly swept off my feet."[17]

It was a scary proposition, but it would be an even bigger shock for others. Hundreds of people were about to be swept not just off their feet—but out of their homes. And little did Michael Dwyer imagine that in two years his new house on Young Avenue would be reduced in value and just living there would be a chore.

CHAPTER 4

BOOSTERS AND NAYSAYERS

The City of Halifax cannot afford…to make a mistake which will be irretrievable, and which will affect the future of its citizens for all time to come.[18]

– Editorial, *Morning Chronicle*

THE RESPONSE FROM THE OTHER LARGE HALIFAX NEWSPAPER, *THE MORNING CHRONICLE*, WAS EQUALLY theatrical. With the *Herald* talking about red blood, the *Chronicle* portrayed the city being laid asunder on Frank Cochrane's operating table. Undertaking this project, the *Chronicle* claimed, "would be no passing or temporary matter—no gentle operation, but a rending asunder of the joints, a dividing of the very bones and marrow of the community."[19]

Assuming their natural stance in opposition to the Conservative government, they vigorously opposed the plan. Against the *Herald*'s gung-ho "Out with the shovels!" attitude, the *Chronicle* assumed a concerned but calm demeanour of sober second thought. Had the situation become so dire that such grim measures as these were called for?

> One of the engineers who helped in the formulation of the new proposition is reported to have said that he was more than surprised at the way in which it had been received by the people in Halifax. He might well be, if he regarded that seeming acceptance as final. What he witnessed, however, was merely an outburst of popular delight over the proposed large expenditure

> for the benefit of Halifax. The scheme itself was scarcely thought of at first. It is only now that sober consideration is being given to the subject. And there are many long and serious thoughts yet to come to the people of Halifax before the matter is finally decided.[20]

From Board of Trade input and a study of the requirements of the steamship companies, railways, and local business, the proposed plan recommended a series of expansions. Additional infrastructure for nine ships would be built post-haste, with accommodation for nine more to be erected three or four years later. Five or six years after that, a further nine vessels would have to be accommodated. Rail capacity would grow in tandem, and ample room for further expansion would be secured.

Cowie and his engineers had scoured the shoreline and narrowed the search to four locations, two on each side of the harbour. All had enough shoreline and depth of water to fit twenty to thirty full-sized steamships of the day at 381-metre-long docks. The first option, which the report dubbed "Scheme A," called for removal of the naval dockyard, a choice sure to cause waves all the way across the Atlantic Ocean to Whitehall. The Royal Navy was gone but they still reserved the right to reoccupy the dockyard if they chose to. Paired with that option was the eradication of downtown Halifax, including the existing waterfront.

These were radical ideas. Perhaps Cowie wanted to show that, in the language of our day, all options were on the table. Things had become so urgent that nothing was beyond consideration.

He then listed the advantages and disadvantages, the main disadvantage being obvious: "Dislocation of established city business with no alternative suitable locations available on the peninsula for the class of business done."[21] With other less drastic consequences to follow, he then concluded with, "Disastrous effect on City Assessment Value and Taxation, at least temporarily."[22] Being so unbelievably complex, it was the most expensive option at $1,235,000 per ship berthing space in 1912 dollars.

So much for Scheme A. Scheme B was across the harbour, running from Tufts Cove, where the power station is now located,

The Halifax waterfront, looking southeast of Pier 2 ca. 1902. [SOURCE UNKNOWN]

approximately to where the Dartmouth ferry has long docked. That was certainly a more sensible option, given that this was mostly empty space with good shoreline and excellent depth. Thirty years previously, the town of Dartmouth, partnering with Canada's largest steamship company, Montréal's Allan Line, had lobbied for a terminal in the area, but Deepwater got built instead. The problem was that access to Dartmouth from Halifax was much more complicated than it is now—and it is complicated enough today with two bridges across The Narrows. About this option the report noted guardedly, "It has been proven over and over again that a harbour located without convenient access from the city and remote from its business centre can never be made successful."[23] It cited a list of examples including Longueuil, QC, across the St. Lawrence River from Montréal, and Birkenhead, England, across the River Mersey from Liverpool. Cost per berth was estimated at $800,000.

That made two unattractive options. On to Scheme C.

Those who still dream that one day the current Ocean Terminals in the South End of Halifax will relocate have actually proposed this one—a move directly across the harbour from where they are now. It would be more difficult to make it happen today, but that area was mostly unsettled in 1912. It went from the south edge of Dartmouth to McNabs Island, at the entrance to Eastern Passage. The estimated cost per steamship berth was $880,000. It also would have been much easier to construct and would have come with most of the benefits that the chosen site had, and fewer of the trade-offs.

That left Scheme D, which extended from Georges Island to Point Pleasant, about which the report noted enthusiastically, "at no Port in the world is there a record of any equal development at anything like an equal expenditure, the natural advantages of the Harbour, the tidal range, the absence of currents or any tendency to silt, and the physical features of the site being unusually favourable both as regards first cost and future maintenance."[24]

Against this, nobody would argue. Experience has also shown that it is the most convenient location for those handling the ships—captains, pilots, tug operators. With competent ship handling to avoid the well-marked reefs in the approaches, it offers a straightforward entry and exit located at the outer part of the harbour. If they got it right, it would be transformational for Halifax. It would bring additional trade and an increased population. A British ship travelling at fourteen knots heading to an available berth could dock, land passengers, and sail again with a loss of little more than four hours. With ICR service, passengers could be in Chicago by the time those sailing on to New York got aboard a train.

Unfortunately, the choice of this area for the Ocean Terminals development would lead to the disappearance of one of the most scenic parts of the peninsula. Nevertheless, they opted for this site. We still cope with it today, and it has grown bigger and uglier over time. Half a century later, like a slow but determined glacier, the docks, railway tracks, and the shipping containers have crept southward, right to the door of Point Pleasant Park. Their presence is all too familiar to the people of Halifax, mainly because to get to their favourite park, which happens to be the city's oldest and best known, they have to cross the biggest and longest of the bridges that span what finally became the product of the Ocean Terminals development. Once there, they have to park next to the ever-expanding container terminal, separated only by a chain link fence from mountains of shipping containers being moved about by gargantuan cranes loading and unloading the largest container ships afloat. The contrast between that scene on their left and the tall, serene trees of the park on the right could not be more stark.

That container terminal was not part of the plan. It came many decades later, but it was a direct outgrowth of Scheme D. Everybody knew there would be unexpected effects, but all they considered were the obvious things that would result from the blasting and digging. Even those clapping, singing, and waving in jubilation at the luncheon knew that cutting a gash wide enough for parallel railway tracks through the centre of a small city like Halifax would have lasting—and unknown—effects. But, as Vito Corleone of *The Godfather* might have said, "It's business."

In his presentation at the Board of Trade luncheon, Cochrane stressed that the impact would be manageable because the trains would be below ground level while travelling through the city. (As things turned out, in some places the train is at ground level and you can see it go by in the neighbourhood, practically in people's backyards. Two bridges are even above ground. At least three times a week I walk *under* the train track—and often under a train hauling upwards of two hundred cars loaded with containers.)

The plan was to dig a big ditch, which would entail a vast amount of blasting, put the tracks on the bottom, and build a total of sixteen bridges so main streets could traverse them. That would definitely entail long-term inconvenience as pedestrians—and, very soon, motorists—would be unable to travel a straight line from point A to point B. It would be like having a deep, unfordable river flowing through the city. The difference is that rivers are attractive and natural and what was being proposed was anything but.

Lots of railway tracks passed through urban areas of Halifax at ground level and people simply looked left and right and then walked across. There was an obvious element of danger, but the vast majority of such pedestrians did it all their lives without harm. It was commonly done with the existing tracks coming into the city alongside The Narrows of the harbour—and had been for half a century. In the scenario presented by Cochrane, the steep walls of the trench would make that impossible. Every time the people of Halifax went anywhere, they would have to find their way to a bridge. In a worst-case scenario, a pedestrian might look across the track/ditch combo straight at their destination less than twenty-five metres away and be forced to walk perhaps half a kilometre to the nearest bridge.

Every single time a train passed, those in the vicinity would know, often because their houses abutted the top of the cut. The clanking of wheels, screeching of brakes, whistles blasting, bells ringing, clouds of steam and coal smoke would be their inevitable companions, day and night. Others would be living alongside a grain elevator, close enough to touch it. The complete relocation of neighbourhoods was on the horizon.

Many questioned whether such a wholesale change to the environment was possible, and there were others who thought the scheme would never come to pass; it was just too ambitious. P. A. Freeman, chief engineer of the Halifax Electric Tramway Company, was concerned that the provision of a critical municipal service was being put in jeopardy. His company, which ran a fleet of what eventually became referred to as streetcars, provided public transportation in the city. They were

Time has shown that the argument that the port would be hemmed in at the current location was correct; today the container shipping business is growing while the container terminal is severely squeezed. The problem has been addressed by building a second container terminal farther into the harbour, where Freeman recommended the docks be built more than a century ago, and by infilling the harbour—the go-to solution for most space problems over the decades. As a consequence, the big harbour that built Halifax keeps getting smaller.

located at the perimeter of the project. That meant, ironically, they would have no space to expand as their company grew. They were about to complete Car Barn no. 4, which would double their capacity, and only days earlier had begun to lay track to the waterfront at the gas company's wharf to enable the ploughing of snow into the harbour.[25]

Freeman argued in *The Morning Chronicle* that in English ports the practice was to locate the docks on the inner parts of a harbour to allow for future expansion. It sounded like the government was about to make the same mistake for the third time.

The same day the *Chronicle* was again pushing its suggestion for a second opinion, George A. MacKenzie, alderman and deputy mayor, wrote to the editor:

> That the Government should recognize the claims of the finest seaport in the world, and resolve to properly equip it for business, must be a satisfaction to every citizen of Halifax, but that the Government have been wrongfully advised is painfully evident.
>
> That the citizens of Halifax will calmly submit to have the city turned upside down, and mercilessly carved up, in a way that neither God nor nature intended, at the will of some engineer who apparently knew nothing, and cared less, about the vital interests of Halifax, is a miracle.[26]

As the general manager of the Acadia Sugar Refinery, the largest business on the waterfront, MacKenzie was well acquainted with managing shipping issues by rail and sea; he dealt daily with the challenges. He then proposed a series of alternatives, some of them no less radical than the one being put forward and, in some ways, no less destructive to the geography of the city.

For his trouble, he was trounced in a letter to *The Morning Chronicle* by Michael Dwyer with good humour and sarcasm, declaring that he had known MacKenzie for many years but had no idea that he was a great engineer.

> In a night, without the assistance of anyone, Alderman George MacKenzie has solved this problem for the City of Halifax and

> for the Government. He has made the engineers who have been engaged in this work for the past nine months look like triflers and children.... Let us demand that the chief engineer in charge of this work be dismissed and replaced by Alderman MacKenzie.[27]

It was a critical challenge for the city, and subsequent newspapers were full of such citizen-on-citizen attacks—the equivalent of today's disputes on social media.

CHAPTER 5

DISAPPEARING THE SHORE

The old railway wharves and yards at Richmond and the deep water terminals are situated on a narrow and restricted foreshore, with inadequate railway connections and with no possibility of any great extensions on economic lines.[28]

– A. C. Brown, Engineer, August 23, 1916

THE TOWN OF HALIFAX WAS PLACED WHERE IT IS FOR TWO REASONS. BOTH HAD TO DO WITH SECURITY— from the weather and from the enemy, during a time of almost constant warfare with the French. After the French colonized Mi'kma'ki, the British took mainland Nova Scotia in 1713, and the French constructed a fortress in Cape Breton they called Louisbourg. That greatly distressed Britain's New England colonies, so London agreed to create an opposing fortress at what they would call Halifax. In the new harbour was a tall hill with a commanding view. They planted the town nearby and built a naval dockyard farther up in the harbour, safe from the weather.

Eight kilometres of shoreline were available between Point Pleasant and the Bedford Basin, but a bend in the shore at South Street exposed the outer 25 percent to weather from the southeast. The town and the waterfront ended at South Street and the shoreline beyond that developed more slowly, becoming instead a place where people went to relax in natural surroundings. There was a swimming area on the beach. Freshwater Brook, a source of fresh water that is now covered, ran from the South Common through the Public Gardens and emptied at the foot of Inglis Street. At twilight, couples often walked along the road to the Kissing Bridge, which needs no explanation. They called the road Pleasant Street. It ran through part of the downtown and out to Point Pleasant.

Today, what remains of that street is called Barrington Street. Thanks to the Ocean Terminals project, it now ends at Inglis. If Barrington were to continue, it would follow the old track of Pleasant Street along the shore as it existed before the development being proposed. Barrington Street north of downtown to North Street was originally called Lockman Street and north of North Street was called Campbell Road. The combination of Pleasant and Lockman Streets and Campbell Road was the only thoroughfare to run the full length of the peninsula, from the Bedford Basin to Point Pleasant. Other streets that would have—Connaught Avenue and Robie Street—got truncated by the railway cut.

The outer part of the area just before Point Pleasant Park was called Green Bank (or Greenbank), named after a point that bulged out from a fairly straight area of shoreline. It was at the bottom of a long, gentle slope that eased its way from high ground at Tower Road down to the shore of the harbour. It was covered with fields, forests, estates, and a few houses. Near the shore, the city had been creeping its way south of Inglis Street toward Point Pleasant and small roads with modest houses had appeared with names like Fawson, Brussels, Plover, and Owen. Above these was Young Avenue, stretching from Inglis to Point Pleasant Park with not-so-modest houses. Named after Sir William Young, who some thirty years earlier had donated the iron gates for a new entrance to the park, it was meant to become the most exclusive street in the city, secured in 1896 by the provincial restrictive covenant that set rules for its development and for the surrounding area.

On that street lived George Campbell, a wealthy shipowner and the driving force behind the building of the Dalhousie University Studley Campus in Halifax. Shipowner W. A. Black also lived there, as did FWW, the city engineer, and Michael Dwyer who, at 11 Young, was uncomfortably close to the planned rail cut. By 1912, Pleasant Street was the most heavily populated street to be affected and included several sizeable properties belonging to successful professionals and

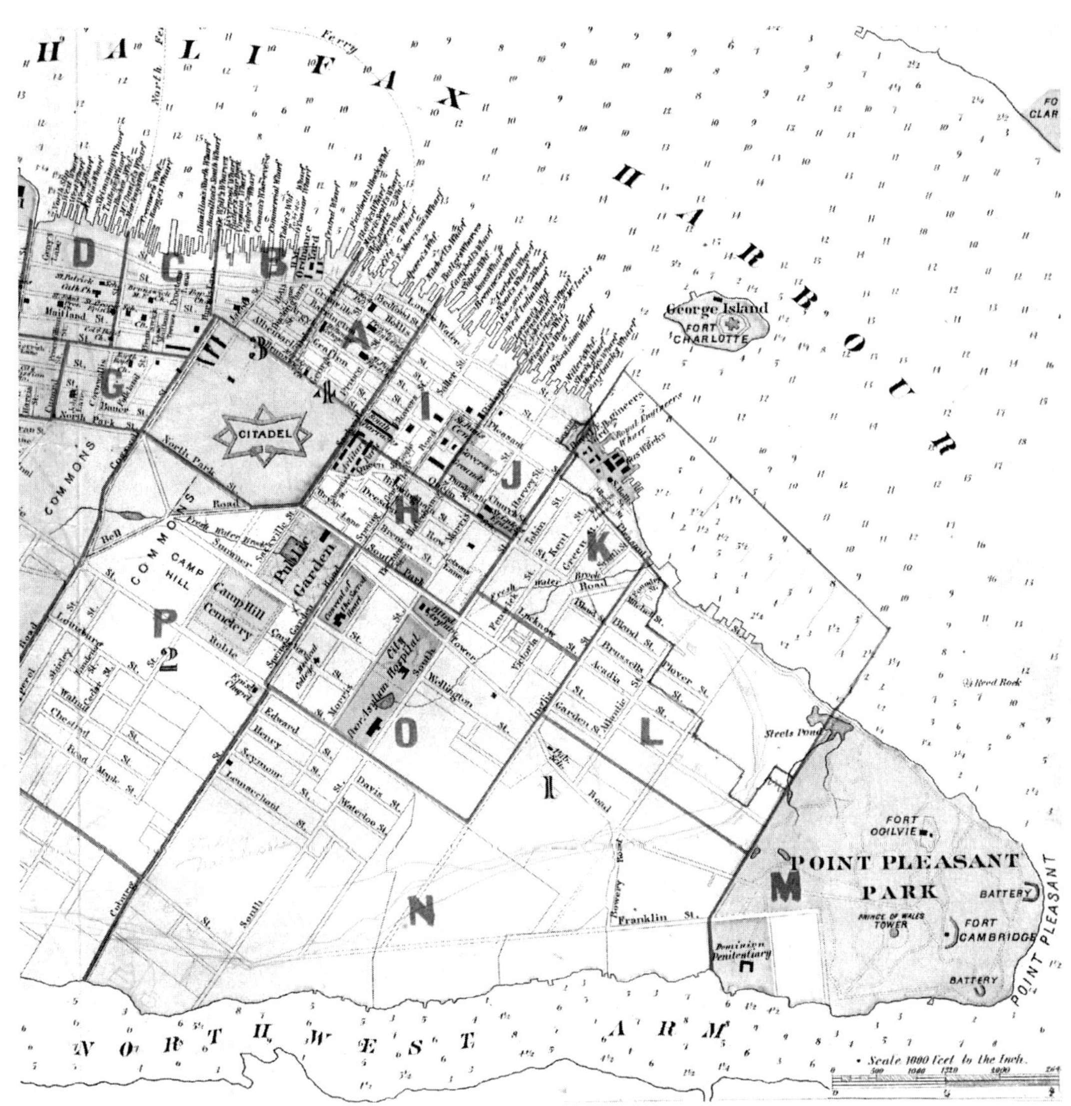

A portion of an 1878 Hopkins City Atlas map of Halifax showing the early layout of Halifax's downtown and South End. Note the crowded downtown waterfront area. The Ocean Terminals were later built along the section of shoreline between downtown and Point Pleasant Park. [H. W. Hopkins NS Archives Library O/S G 1129 H3 H67 1878]

businessmen like builder Samuel Brookfield, Hugh R. Silver, who was instrumental in getting the *Bluenose* built in 1921, and brewer George W. C. Oland, whose house was occupied by his estranged wife, Ella Young Bauld. Her widowed mother, Mrs. H. G. Bauld, lived next door. The area was the result of unplanned growth, a bit of a patchwork with several neighbourhoods, one of which was industrial and had a gas plant that extracted gas from coal for domestic use. The gas was piped around the downtown and used for cooking, lighting, and heating. There had always been light industry in the area, and there was a working-class neighbourhood for those employed nearby.

At the foot of Inglis Street, the city had placed a seawall in the 1860s with a park, benches, and walking area called the Esplanade. When the Ocean Terminals project began, the contractors took over the popular site, prompting the city to evaluate it at $50,000 and submit a claim for remuneration.

At the southern extremity of the original waterfront, the three main streets there today—Water, Hollis, and Barrington—take an abrupt right turn one after the other as they confront the Westin Nova Scotian, which began as the Nova Scotian Hotel when it was later built as part of the project. In 1912 that area was where the seashore bent toward Point Pleasant, forcing Lower Water and Hollis each into a turn. Few people, including those who have lived there all their lives, appreciate what an upheaval took place in that part of the city and how much the natural lay of the land got altered with the building of the Ocean Terminals. The entire area of the harbour from modern-day South Street to the lower parking lot at Point Pleasant would eventually be infilled, in some places running out into the harbour close to half a kilometre.

After the luncheon at The Halifax, the whole area between Inglis and Point Pleasant soared in stature. *The Morning Chronicle* and other naysayers rose in righteous indignation that this veritable Eden would be sacrificed to extend the port. However, this Eden had over the years also been home to a tannery, a foundry, a brewery, some distilleries, a lobster packing plant, a fish-smoking plant, and, for seventy years, the gas plant. William Montgomery even built locomotives there, even though delivering each new engine to the railway required laying temporary tracks through downtown out to Deepwater to connect

Starting in the 1960s, a long period of decline set in at the Halifax waterfront, as the mainstay activities of shipping, fishing, and coastal transportation changed and, bit by bit, the local operators ceased to exist. Today the original waterfront, the defining area of the city for two centuries with its jumble of wharves big and small, where passenger liners, fishing schooners, tugboats, ferries, coal barges, and other vessels came and went, is no more—replaced by a boardwalk, which is enormously popular with Haligonians and visitors and is very much alive. It's visited each year by massive numbers of people who enjoy soaking up the history and the sun, swilling boutique beer, downing everything from hot dogs to lobster, and marvelling at the overwhelming ships that appear out of nowhere, barely disturbing the water, and silently slither by on their ways to the military dockyard, Richmond Terminals, the Coast Guard base, Fairview Cove container terminal, the gypsum pier, and the naval ammunition magazine, or toward anchorage in the Bedford Basin.

The railway depots—Richmond, Ocean Terminals, and the two container terminals—have since become the dominant commercial occupants in the harbour.

with the tracks of the customer, the ICR. A resident of Pleasant Street reminded readers of the *Herald* that "the larger part of the shore on the proposed site is, and has been for years, the only really dirty part of our harbor."[29] That was because of a big, fat sewer outlet that was around until the city got a wastewater treatment plant in 2008.

The naysayers' dread of Point Pleasant Park being ransacked led them to purport that any docks erected on this exposed shore would be short-lived, trotting out horror stories of damage by storms past. Cochrane had already thought that through and included the construction of a breakwater on the outer side of the development to shelter the docks. It would be built on the harbour side of Point Pleasant Park and extend through reasonably shallow water out past Reid's Rock, which lay offshore. Well, they grumbled, that would never work! A breakwater would cause the harbour to freeze in winter, demoting it from its elevated status as an ice-free harbour. The natural flow of the tides would be disrupted, slowing the currents that kept the waters in motion, inhibiting ice formation. In fact, the breakwater was nowhere near long enough to do that. And it is not the tides that inhibit the ice in the harbour; it is the bone-chilling winds that blast out of the north in winter. Anybody who lives on the Northwest Arm is aware that any ice that forms in the Arm in the dead of winter ultimately gets blown out before it can melt in spring.

When the Ocean Terminals project concluded, the eight-kilometre eastern side of the peninsula was fully developed. It was such a perfect interface between land and sea that it just had to be put to use. The northerly migration of docks and other marine infrastructure began with the waterfront, which served the town below the citadel, starting in 1749. Then to its north came the naval dockyard, completed in 1759. Farther north the railroads got established with tracks and docks in the 1850s, and finally the Halifax Shipyard, used for shipbuilding and repair, in the 1880s.

By then, the Deep Water Terminus, which came about in 1880 to bolster the Richmond docks, was showing its age. Deepwater had been built with a big budget of federal money. In meeting their commitment for a rail connection from upper Canada to Halifax, the federal government had automatically created a need for more shipping infrastructure.

Pier 2 was the first to be rebuilt. At least one generation of concrete docks was replaced, as evidenced by the slabs of concrete I encountered on the bottom while looking for bottles and chinaware from the ships that frequented the area. During the Second World War the Canadian Navy took over the facility and eventually integrated it into HMC Dockyard. Pier 2 was absorbed in 1971 and replaced by a new jetty in 1996.

The piers were made of wood and took a lot of wear and tear from ships coming and going; rain, ice, and sun beating down; supporting the weight of loaded trains; and of course, fire. They were eventually rebuilt with concrete and were used for many decades.

Before Cochrane's Ocean Terminals announcement at the Board of Trade luncheon in 1912, rumours were rampant, and when it came, sharp-witted operators started beating a path to property owners' doors looking to purchase and then flip their acquisitions to the richest organization in the country—the federal government. Others who thought they should have been in the know were miffed because they had been left out and missed an opportunity.

James MacGregor's situation was typical. He ran a grocery store at the corner of Morris and Pleasant (now called Barrington) Streets. He was approached and asked to put a price on his store and the two houses adjoining. The so-called agent suggested $15,000 and, as MacGregor declined to put a price on his property, the "agent" kept raising his offer in $5,000 increments until he got to $35,000. Still MacGregor protested that he didn't care to sell, and the agent left, only to return inside of an hour to make a final offer of $45,000. Unknown to the agent, Morris Street would be outside the development zone—so not all of the intended speculation returned a profit.

Investment banker J. C. Mackintosh observed that twelve to fourteen locals, both Conservative and Liberal, had been kept in the know as the plans came together.[30] One Tory party source reportedly noted, "There's at least a million in it for the 'insiders.'"[31] That prompted a statement, on behalf of the government, from lawyers W. A. Henry and T. F. Tobin that "the purchases [of property] which are reported to have been made and the options which are reported to have been given at prices greatly in excess of current values were NOT negotiated by the government, or by any one with the government's authority."[32]

According to authors Steven Schwinghamer and Jan Raska in *Pier 21: A History*, "the manipulation of real estate prices did lead to numerous claims proceeding through the Exchequer Court (which dealt with federal cases) and to the Supreme Court. This process stretched into the mid-1920s, long after the foundation of the Ocean Terminals and the associated rail cut were completed."[33]

CHAPTER 6

THE RAILWAY VERSUS CITY HALL

The influence of the railway lobby has a very long reach. Many cities of the Pacific Coast have had their experiences with railroads who wished to go about things their own way.[34]

– Deputy Mayor George MacKenzie

WHILE EVERYBODY WAS SPECULATING ABOUT PROPERTIES CHANGING HANDS AND WHO WAS GETTING RICH, those tasked with keeping order and protecting the interests of the citizens had much to worry about. The city had invested taxpayers' money in services such as streets, sidewalks, lighting, water, and sewage facilities that would soon be destroyed. Dislodged residents would be moved to other places in the city where such services would have to be created all over again. Who was going to pay for that? Two weeks after the announcement, nobody from the federal government or the railways had been in touch with City Hall to set their minds at ease.

Along with that, neighbouring properties not required for the terminals and yards were bound to become uninhabitable or unfit for use, leading to a reduction in value. The tax revenue on those lands would be lost. In 1910, the City of Halifax had $24.6 million worth of assessable property. Two fifths, or $9.2 million worth of Imperial, Dominion, provincial, county, educational, charitable, church, and other organizations' properties were non-taxable.[35] The city could ill afford to lose a large chunk of the remainder. The mayor and councillors had good reason to be lying awake at night.

On November 18, 1912, Halifax City Council met to discuss a report of the Civic Improvement League on what the announcement would mean for the city. Eight aldermen supported the project; four did not.[36] The vote was a clear indication of support at City Hall, but, like the boosters, they did not have any sense of the full picture. The job now was to get connected and stay on top of what was going to be a big part of their lives for the foreseeable future.

The report's first recommendation was that City Council ask the Dominion government to allow Council to be involved in the development planning so they could ensure that the city's interests were taken into account. The report also suggested a landscape architect be included to guide the development along aesthetic lines, proposing the distinguished British landscape architect Thomas H. Mawson as a good option based on his work designing the boulevard leading to Dalhousie University. Mawson was of national renown, having completed commissions in Toronto, Vancouver, Banff, and Victoria; he would go on to complete others for Regina, Saskatoon, and Calgary.

But Cochrane knew better. He responded to this recommendation in a letter to council read December 6, advising the aldermen that he had the matter in hand and there would be no need for a landscape architect. The minister had the last word; council's participation in design efforts affecting their own city would not be required. And so it went.

Then came the main issue pertaining to the hundreds of thousands of dollars (tens of millions in today's dollars) invested by the city in the permanent infrastructure—which the city called "works"—that would be destroyed during construction and have to be reconstructed elsewhere. The council sought reassurance that when the plans were finally settled and the costs for damage calculated the government would reimburse the city.

Seven months later, on June 17, 1913—six weeks before the project started—Frank Cochrane was in Halifax with the prime minister. Along with the new general manager of Government Railways Frederick Gutelius (a Pennsylvania civil engineer new to this role after fifteen years with the CPR), ICR General Superintendent F. P. Brady, and Frederick Cowie, the group met with the Board of Control and City Engineer FWW Doane. Mayor Edward Williams of Dartmouth also attended.

Francis William Whitney (FWW) Doane, who served as Halifax city engineer from 1891 to 1924. [Halifax Municipal Archives 102-5-1-84.8]

The outcome was that FWW and Gutelius would confer further regarding the restoration of and compensation for the city's sewers and sidewalks. It so happened that FWW, in his previous job, had gained significant experience in building railroads in Nova Scotia, so he and Gutelius had a connection. It turned out that the costs of lost city infrastructure had been dealt with in the House of Commons on May 13, when Frank Cochrane had been questioned and had replied that such expenses would be covered in the budget. Nobody had bothered to advise the city.

The railways were used to getting their way. On July 10, 1913, a frustrated W. J. Clayton, a successful clothing manufacturer and landowner whose property would one day become the Clayton Park neighbourhood of Halifax, wrote to the mayor of Halifax about a level crossing on Campbell Road, what today is North Barrington Street. He had just experienced a collision between his automobile and a train.

> I have, upon several occasions, called the attention of the City Engineer to the dangerous condition of Campbell Road.... This piece of roadway is very narrow, with two very dangerous level crossings, at short distances apart and with main tracks of railway on each side in almost continuous use by trains and engines.... I understand that Campbell Road is supposed to be and was originally a street sixty (60) feet wide, but the railways have been permitted to narrow it at different times and now portions of the roadway are only eighteen (18) feet wide.

A similar situation had occurred in the same area more than thirty years before Clayton wrote his letter. The offending place was in the city's industrial north end. Bound for the sugar refinery, Hillis & Sons Foundry, the Dominion Textile plant, the shipyard, and the railway yards, workers arrived on the north ferry from Dartmouth six mornings a week and had to cross railway tracks morning and evening. In 1915, James McGregor observed that at one location near the North Street Station more than fifty engine movements occurred every hour as railway cars got shunted around.

It went on for decades. When Haligonian Bernie McCorry was a boy living on North Barrington Street in the 1930s, he regularly took a shortcut by climbing up and down a three-metre wall when going to and from the shoreline. Because he loved roaming the docks and talking to the men working there, it was an easy trip for him. He descended the vertical concrete wall using iron spikes that somebody had driven in. At the bottom, he crossed a dozen sets of tracks to get to the docks. Later, when he worked at the dockyard, he crossed five or six sets of tracks twice daily on his way to and from work.

In response to Clayton's complaint, City Clerk Fred Monaghan sent a fawning letter to Frederick Gutelius: "The Board of Control desire to urge upon the management of the I.C.R. the necessity of abolishing the level crossings at the points referred to in Clayton's letter and earnestly request that you will take the matter up as soon as possible."[37]

"Desire"; "urge upon"; "earnestly request"; "as soon as possible"—not exactly hard-hitting. In its dealings with the city, the railway had a habit of throwing its weight around, making decisions and then informing council—or not. Sometimes the railway folks simply decided on a course of action and left it up to council to discover what they were up to. It had always been thus.

The Deep Water Terminus had just been completed, and the railway tracks needed to be extended to the new docks. It was a tight space, so they would have to run along the east side of Water Street, sharing some of the roadbed. In May 1881 the city and the ICR drew up an agreement. A year later the railway let the city know that they were ready to get started and handed the city engineer a new plan that called for the tracks to be laid within the surface of Water Street for a distance

259 metres farther than stated in the agreement. Horses, wagons, pedestrians, *and trains* would be sharing the same thoroughfare for a quarter of a kilometre. It was a disaster waiting to happen.

They worked it out in court, but the account demonstrates the headaches civil engineers faced along the shore of The Narrows, with the dockyard on one side and, on the other side, the freight sheds backed up against the hills. The peninsula is a bit like a turtle's back, high in the centre with a steep grade down to the water all around. Having to embed parts of the railway track into the road is evidence of how tight it was. Competition for road space between automobile and train was only going to increase.

The Board of Control was a short-lived experiment in civic politics, consisting of the mayor and four controllers, all elected officials. It was an attempt to solve some of the problems that afflicted many fast-growing North American cities in the early twentieth century. Pushed by the powerful Board of Trade under Michael Dwyer, it sought to make the running of the city more businesslike and less political. The result was a City Council reduced from 18 to 12 councillors and drained of much of its power, which was vested in the hands of the more executive-like Board of Control. Henry Roper, in his book *The Halifax Board of Control: The Failure of Municipal Reform, 1906–1919*, noted, "Board of control supporters argued that it was business-like, progressive and efficient; the establishment of a paid executive would make possible the many changes that were needed to create a better city, and the principal obstacle to change, the aldermen, would be limited in their ability to obstruct."[115]

The new system, which came into being with the election of April 30, 1913, existed during the time of most intense activity on the Ocean Terminals project and was challenged by the unique problems the controllers had to confront. While they were grappling with difficult issues such as a long and violent tramway strike, the First World War, and the Halifax Explosion, they were dogged by complaints arising from the Ocean Terminals project, issues they were usually powerless to fix. It was not a project of their creation nor one they were obliged to correct, but ignoring it was not an option either. The Board of Control was finally voted out in a plebiscite attached to the election of April 30, 1919, and the aldermanic system returned.

CHAPTER 7

EVERYBODY OUT!

Borden and the Tories had delivered for the Maritimes. Halifax businessmen now had to prove that their port was worthy of such government favour; it came down to a decision of which they valued more, their businesses or their homes.[38]

– Murray Hodgins, MA thesis, 1992

THE FIRST ORDER OF BUSINESS WAS TO MAP THE ROUTE. THE EXISTING TRACK, DATING FROM THE DAYS OF the Nova Scotia Railway, takes a ninety-degree left turn to enter the city at the south end of the Basin, skirting the shore to The Narrows under the MacKay Bridge into Halifax. The new route would ignore that turn and head straight to the Arm, travelling 2.5 kilometres to cross the isthmus to Quinpool Road. After that, conditions became complicated by rugged terrain and landowners licking their lips in anticipation of sweet deals. By March 7, 1913, the route was laid down and the specifications released under the signature of the chief engineer for Canadian Government Railways (CGR), James McGregor (not the James MacGregor with the store on Morris Street). He would manage the project for the Government of Canada.

With language that begins, "All these certain lots, pieces or parcels of land hereinafter more particularly described by reference to the center line of the said railway..." the document is impossible to read by anybody except a surveyor or engineer. The *Herald*'s interpretation is easier to navigate for those familiar with the area.

> The line of the railway survey along the Arm reaches Quinpool Road through the Flinn property [today called Flinn Park], passes under Quinpool Road, takes off the northeast corner of Armdale, the property of Sir Charles Tupper, crosses Prince Arthur Street, then crosses the southern portion of Pinehurst, the property of Robert O'Mullin. The continuation of the line passes directly through the house of S. R. Cossey on Pryor Street, then through Jubilee property southeasterly, cutting off part of Jubilee cottage....

The route continued south with the Arm on the right, traversing Coburg and South Streets, where it began a sweeping left turn across the peninsula, nearing Point Pleasant Park and ending near the area across from Georges Island. Laying track along the seashore is the preferred practice for railroad builders because it's level. Cowie, the designer of the line, created the myth that they did not follow the route along the shore of the Arm because they did not want to destroy the natural beauty of the area. In fact, they needed to make the railbed rise gradually to get over a high point on the way to the end of the line, which was on the other side of the peninsula where the docks of the Ocean Terminals would be located. The highest point was at Tower Road, where they blasted and dug the deepest excavation of the whole trench and built the highest bridge of the project.

Land expropriations occurred at both ends of the route and everywhere in between. At the locations where the sixteen bridges were scheduled to be erected, the expropriations swelled to allow for the increased construction activity at those locations. Whole streets disappeared and mansions were levelled. The estates of some Halifax bluebloods—with names like The Oaks, The Bower, and Blenheim—got cut in two or had corners lobbed off. On Prince Arthur Drive off Quinpool Road, the home where Prime Minister Robert Borden lived for fifteen years while he was a Halifax lawyer now looms high above the tracks. The tenants of the apartments can look down and see the container trains sliding by. Nearby, Prime Minister Sir Charles Tupper's Armdale estate lost a piece of its backyard, and trains now trundle along behind the six-car garage. That neighbourhood is now called Armdale, after the estate.

The most significant casualty to Halifax's built heritage was Oaklands, the estate of Samuel Cunard's second son, William, built in 1865. In 1904, William had been obliged to move to England to assume control of the Cunard Steamship Company following the death of his older brother Edward. Roderick Macdonald bought the estate and the lavish thirty-seven room house for $23,500 and had owned it for ten years when the government expropriated it.

Four hundred 25-metre-tall centuries-old trees had already been cut and the land was slated to be ravaged with dynamite and steam shovels when the government auctioned the house with the caveat that it had to be moved. Board of Trade president F. B. McCurdy snapped it up for $1,250—basically a giveaway for the finest house in Atlantic Canada. With a deal like that, McCurdy didn't mind spending $15,000 for a Chicago company to move the twenty-eight-by-fourteen–metre

Pinehurst on Prince Arthur Drive was built for John DeWolf in 1873. Robert Borden owned it from 1893 to 1908. Today it is a set of apartments. [NS Archives photographic collection]

three-storey mansion half a kilometre over rough terrain to Marlborough Woods. But his dream went up in smoke. With the move scheduled and the house looming nearly two metres in the air on a steel frame supported by two hundred jacks, it caught fire and burned during the night of December 28, 1914. Fuelled by an interior of well-seasoned mahogany, walnut, and cherry, the building was too far from a fire hydrant and the firefighters were helpless to even slow the fire's progress. By 1:00 A.M. on the 29th, the whole thing was in ruins.

It could not have been rebuilt for under $150,000 in 1914 dollars, making it worth twice the value of the biggest expropriation payout made by the federal government. Left to mark its existence is Oakland Road, which led from the house on the Arm to Robie Street, where the iron gates and entrance to the estate still stand surrounding the porter's house.

At $76,500, the richest payout went to Samuel Brookfield for Brookhurst, his Pleasant Street home near the shore at the corner of Pleasant and Owen Streets. Brookfield moved to Young Avenue to be closer to his son John. The aging entrepreneur also received $1,800 for several lots at Marlborough Woods near the Northwest Arm, $1,500 for a second batch at the same location, and $750 for property on Plover Street. He was also negotiating for $2,250 in return for a Brussels Street property.

It's not surprising to learn he had a very nice house given that he was the foremost builder in Nova Scotia and perhaps all of Atlantic Canada, having constructed a large sugar refinery in Halifax and another in Dartmouth, a textile mill on the corner of Robie and Young Streets, and, conceivably his best-known achievement, the Memorial Tower, colloquially known as the Dingle, a stone tower that still stands in Sir Sandford Fleming Park. In 1887, he and five others from Halifax founded the Eastern Canada Savings and Loan Company, a financial services firm that was around for a century. Brookfield's most ambitious project was the construction and management of the Halifax Graving Dock, a dry dock that serves as a ship maintenance and repair facility for the Royal Canadian Navy's East Coast fleet, and which survives while still making money for the Halifax Shipyard almost a century and a half later.

The streets of Halifax's South End in the early 1900s. Pleasant Street, which no longer exists, is visible along the shoreline. The site of the Halifax Golf Club is now Gorsebrook Park. [NS ARCHIVES MAP COLLECTION: V6 240]

The Royal Nova Scotia Yacht Squadron, one of the oldest yacht clubs on the continent, had its clubhouse nearby, about halfway between the modern-day Westin Nova Scotian and Point Pleasant Park. The squadron, as it is still called in yachting circles, had been at its location since 1890, after it had been forced in 1876 to board up the first clubhouse in The Narrows for lack of money and had gone without a fixed location. Now, after twenty-two years, it had to move again. With three years' notice, the clubhouse was taken over in 1915 and the club moved into temporary quarters compliments of their neighbour, Samuel Brookfield. The squadron built another clubhouse to the south, and on July 15, 1922, it moved into its fourth home, located on what is now the lower parking lot at Point Pleasant Park.

To expedite the expropriations, the Eastern Trust Company acted as agents for the federal government and processed the payments through the Bank of Nova Scotia. R. H. Fraser, the right-of-way and lease agent for the Department of Railways and Canals, appointed Melvin Clarke, with two other real estate evaluators, W. S. Rogers and J. S. Harris, to calculate what each affected property was worth and determine what the government would pay. All three independently evaluated each property and came to agreement on the value. Fraser submitted the details of ninety-seven properties to be expropriated, which the prime minister signed on December 25, 1913—Christmas Day.

That number would triple by the time the last one was settled, years after the project was completed. In testimony regarding one of the cases that ended up in court, Clarke attested that the majority of owners were satisfied with their evaluations and sold their properties when the government came calling. Not all did, though. At least thirty ended up in the Exchequer Court of Canada, some dragging on into the 1920s before finally being settled. One was the Roman Catholic Episcopal Corporation of Halifax, which owned eight acres where the bridge on Quinpool Road was built. They had planned to establish an infants' home there, but the rail cut messed up their plans and they had to build it elsewhere.

The Auditor General reported that, up to March 13, 1914, the government had made payments for 109 properties totalling $796,548,51.[39] There were still 57 properties on which the government

William Cunard's Oaklands estate in happier days, before it was destroyed by fire in 1914. [NOTMAN STUDIO NS ARCHIVES ACCESSION NO. 1983-310 NO. 50203]

Brookhurst, on Pleasant Street, was one of the most significant houses to be expropriated and destroyed in service of the rail cut. [SOURCE UNKNOWN]

had made offers that had not yet been accepted, and 43 other properties including valuable ones like Oaklands for which no offers had yet been made.

For $282.50, J. J. Skerry sold a Victoria Lane property on 48 square metres, probably the smallest of all. At the other extreme, Alex Wilson, with a fish market and buildings covering an area of more than 60,409 square metres, had not yet settled. C. W. Anderson sold 60,669 metres of vacant land on Jubilee Road for $30,000.

Most were modest homes belonging to working-class folk like Ellen Kelly at 8 Gas Lane, who sold her little dwelling on 334 metres for $3,000, and Thomas Doull, who got $1,500 for his house on just 192 metres on South Hollis Street. Many claims were for multiple properties. With eight, Arthur Boutilier submitted the most claims, all pertaining to properties in the Green Bank area. He was aiming for a total of $76,641, with no luck thus far. He ended up in court where it was revealed that he had inside information provided by John R. McLeod, who had been present when details of the project had been divulged to an inner circle that included Michael Dwyer, George Campbell, and others prior to the announcement.[40] Pleasant Street was the longest street to disappear, with a record fifty-six payouts. Pleasant Avenue also vanished, with twenty-six, and Plover Street lost twenty-two homes. The smallest payment was $150 for a property in Purcells Cove, one of four associated with quarrying granite for the docks. All told, there were perhaps 275 to 300 claims submitted and the government paid out about $1.5 to $2 million—$45 million in today's currency.

Table 7-1: Properties purchased by the federal government to make way for the rail cut; see Appendix A for the names of those whose properties were expropriated.

Street	Buyouts	Comment
Albert Street	1	Gone; the street name has been reused in Halifax's North End.
Atlantic Street	10	Shortened; runs today between Tower Road and South Bland Street.

Bayers Road	3	Required for a bridge to cross the tracks at Bayers Road.
Bower Road	4	Altered to merge with Rogers Drive.
Brussels Street	4	Now runs between Inglis and Atlantic Streets.
Chebucto Road	1	Train tracks pass over Chebucto Road.
Clarence Street	1	All that remains is now Harbourview Drive between Young Avenue and Tower Road.
Coburg Road	7	Required for a bridge on Coburg Road.
Dutch Village Road	3	Now Joseph Howe Avenue.
Fairview/ Bedford Road	10	These properties were taken to build the rail yard beside the Bedford Highway.
Fawson Road	5	Now Terminal Road.
Gas Lane	3	Gone.
Hollis Street	3	Unchanged.
Jubilee Road	2	Runs over the tracks to the Northwest Arm.
Marlborough Woods	9	Now a subdivision.
Miller Road	1	Now Point Pleasant Drive.
Miller Subdivision	1	Gone; was once the location of Green Bank neighbourhood; now part of the container terminal storage yard near Point Pleasant.
Mumford Road	2	Required for a raised bridge on Mumford Road over the cut.
NW Arm & Jubilee Road	1	C. W. Anderson got $30,000 for much of the Jubilee estate.
Oakland Road	1	Required for a bridge on Oakland Road.
Owen Street	3	Southwood Drive, between Young and Tower, is all that remains.
Oxford Street	1	n/a
Pleasant Avenue	26	Gone.

Pleasant Street	56	Gone; Barrington now ends at Inglis; it used to be called Pleasant Street and ran past Inglis along the shore to Point Pleasant Park.
Plover Street	22	Gone.
Pryor Street	1	n/a
Purcells Cove Quarry	4	n/a
Quinpool Road	7	Required for bridge on Quinpool Road.
Skerry Place	4	Gone.
South Hollis Street	9	Gone.
South Street	4	South Street touches the project at both ends—at a bridge near the Arm and at the Nova Scotian Hotel near the waterfront.
Tower Road	3	The bridge over Tower Road is the highest of all the bridges built.
Victoria Lane	9	Now Victoria Road.
Young Avenue	6	The Young Avenue bridge is the longest of all the bridges built.
Other	11	Unable to identify the locations of these claims.

From the start, F. H. Bell, the city solicitor, had been opposed to the Ocean Terminals project, even declaring his opposition in a letter to *The Halifax Chronicle*. He was concerned that the loss of tax revenue from such a large number of expropriated properties that would become tax-free under federal ownership would have to be replaced or the city would have to raise property taxes—always an undesirable option. Nobody knew for sure how big the project was going to be, but $1 million was a number that got thrown around in terms of potential loss from the property tax rolls. At the time, the total taxable property in the city was about $19 million, so that would have been a big shortfall for the taxpayers of the day to make up.

In February of 1914, Bell showed signs of being a prophet when Mayor Fred Bligh received a letter from railway lawyer T. F. Tobin advising that a slate of expropriated properties assessed at $660,650 had been filed at the Registry of Deeds. There would be more because the government was at that time still negotiating for many additional properties. He went on to note, "In view of the fact that property owned by the Crown is exempt under the provisions of the City Charter, I would ask you to kindly take the matter up and advise me what course will be adopted by the City."

The mayor immediately took the matter up with the local MP, who happened to be the prime minister. Robert Borden's prompt reply: "The representations sent forth in your communication will have the careful consideration of the Government."[41] The government agreed to pay the current property taxes as well as those for any other properties up to the point when the residents moved out and the railway took possession. After that, it was up to the city to find a way to replace the revenue.

Blenheim Lodge, which is still a private home in Halifax, was once the home of Sir Sandford Fleming, the chief engineer on the building of the Intercolonial Railway. Ironically, Fleming had to plead with the city to spare it from demolition during the construction of the rail cut. [COURTESY GRAEME HIGGS]

Three years later it was still a problem for the city. All the properties that the railway decided they needed had been purchased, but had not all been put to use, so the federal government decided to rent them out. On Pleasant Street they had multiple rental properties with a total of $255,000 in unpaid property taxes, with more on Atlantic Street and Young Avenue, for a total of $295,000. It greatly irked the city fathers that untaxed military, naval, railway, and other federal properties were all over the place in their city, but to have the federal government acting as a tax-free landlord collecting rent on the properties was a bit much.

In May of 1913, with work soon to begin, Sir Sandford Fleming, the chief engineer on the building of the ICR, sent a message to the Halifax mayor with the ironic news that his house near the Arm was slated to come down. He reminded the mayor that he had donated ninety-five acres of land to the city for a park on the Arm—still there—and was now looking for help to avoid losing his house. The mayor responded that he had no authority in the matter and could not help. Fleming put in two claims for an unspecified amount pertaining to property on Oxford Street, just above his house, and on South Street, south of his estate. The house, called Blenheim Lodge, which William Duffus built in 1871, and which Fleming called Summer House when he acquired it in 1872, survived—but barely, as the cut passes it less than thirty metres away. Between 1998 and 2017, property developer Graeme Higgs owned it. He told me that at that time an average of six trains a day went by without making enough noise to be a bother.

Some of the structures purchased were demolished immediately; others were left for the time being or occupied by the contractors, and others were auctioned at fire-sale prices and moved elsewhere. On May 15, 1914, fifty-two transactions were consummated for single or multiple buildings on properties, most needing to be moved. On May 27, another nineteen were sold. On that day, a two-storey house measuring ten metres by nine metres that the government had purchased from C. C. Morton at 9 South Street for $6,150 sold for two hundred dollars, which was at the top of the price curve. The lowest price for a building that day was seven dollars. It would be interesting to know if anybody sold their house and then bought it back at a lower price and moved it.

To move a house, council required a minimum twenty-dollar deposit for repairs to the road. Most were short moves from places like Pleasant Street to lots just outside the construction zone, but others were farther afield. On July 10, 1914, the Board of Control met to consider an application from realtors McCallum's Limited to move two houses from 10 and 12 South Hollis Street to a lot on Chebucto Road, a minimum of two kilometres. That would have been a big undertaking. The Civic Improvement League, founded in 1906 by the Board of Trade to advocate for the planned and orderly development of the city, opposed the move, as did D. Lorne McGibbon and others who lived in the target neighbourhood. It took three meetings and many presentations before the controllers finally rejected the request and instructed the company to not move any more houses to Chebucto Road.

Because the trucks of the day were greatly underpowered compared to today, horses provided the power to move a house. It began with raising the house using screw jacks and constructing a sled beneath on which the house would ride. Then, a wooden track of greased planks was put down on the street for the sled to slide over. As the horses leaned into the haul, and the house inched along the street, the planks and ties left behind were picked up and placed at the front of the house and used over and over. Sometimes pulleys connected to an immoveable object like a tree or anchor were also used.

The big houses on Young Avenue were not exempt from all this. The widest cut of the project went through that lightly populated but influential street. On February 25, 1916, the Ocean Terminals Railway received approval to move C. Ochiltree Macdonald's house, which had been boarded up since February 1914, from 34 Young Avenue, and to move Louisa Smith's house at 35 Young Avenue across Owen Street, which was about to be swallowed into the cut.

By February 1914, the need to alter the directions of some Halifax streets began to crop up. Mumford Road would have to be changed to cross the proposed railway line at closer to a right angle. That meant expropriating the land over which the new part of the road would run. It also took the road out of commission for a time, which necessitated effort from the city solicitor to get the contractors to provide alternate routes for Haligonians. Bayers Road was in the same situation.

It was soon determined that the owners of the Mumford Road land, the St. Patrick's Home for Boys, were not satisfied with what the city was offering for the land. Section 688 of the city charter therefore required each party to nominate an arbitrator. The process ground on. To avoid arbitration, the city made a new offer. The trustees of the home counter-offered. The city stalled. Eventually, in the winter of 1916, they came to terms—two years after they had started.

For those affected, the messy expropriations and forced moves were bad enough, but those challenges paled in comparison to the upheaval the construction phase would bring.

At left (with scaffolding), is Pine Grove, the Young Avenue home of Mrs. Louisa Martin Smith, on October 2, 1916. Behind that is C. Ochiltree Macdonald's mansion. Both houses had to be moved to avoid being swallowed into the rail cut. [Halifax Municipal Archives, Gauvin & Gentzel photograph (CR6-122.272)]

CHAPTER 8
GETTING UP STEAM

The City of Halifax cannot afford…to make a mistake which will be irretrievable, and which will affect the future of its citizens for all time to come.

– Editorial, *Halifax Morning Chronicle*

IN LESS THAN A WEEK AFTER FRANK COCHRANE'S OCTOBER 30, 1912, ANNOUNCEMENT, SURVEYORS WERE seen at the Northwest Arm near the Waegwoltic Club and the Birchdale Hotel at the bottom of Coburg Road. That caused some angst, which Frederick Gutelius was quick to quell. He used the occasion to also reassure worried promoters of higher education, led by George Campbell, that the Studley property, where Dalhousie University would soon rise, would not be affected.

The Canadian winter provided ample time for the rumour mill to chug along. There was talk that, because of pushback at the planned cut across the city, the tracks would go instead along the other side of the Arm. A bridge would then take the trains across to the South End of the city and into the terminals. A bridge across the Arm? Never! What had been described was already bad enough. Others heard that a railway hotel was planned for the corner of Spring Garden Road and South Park Street, where the Lord Nelson Hotel sits today. There was even talk of a "West End Station"—a railway station south of Jubilee Road on the Arm.[42] It never came to fruition, but rumours about the hotel were surprisingly prescient.

Two months after Frank Cochrane's announcement, the construction of the new Pier 2 began a couple of kilometres farther north. It was big and broad-shouldered, able to support 128,000 tons on its surface, and had four sets of railway tracks running onto it. It also featured a modern immigration facility in a double-storeyed shed. Upon completion, it would provide essentially the same things that the Ocean Terminals piers would feature, but on a smaller scale. It was meant as one part of an update to Deepwater. When Ocean Terminals got rolled out, Halifax would end up with two new immigration facilities. On top of that, the Ocean Terminals project called for a new grain elevator because that was where all the freighters would be docking and loading. Contractor M. E. Keefe had just replaced the grain elevator at Deepwater with a new one nearly fifty metres tall with capacity of half a million bushels.

This new pier was being erected where Samuel Cunard had built his six wharves many decades before. The contractor commenced work on January 2, 1913. On that day, the first of 1,818 reinforced concrete posts called pilings, which the Nova Scotia Construction Company had fabricated at their plant in Eastern Passage, were driven into the sea floor. It was a leading-edge construction method that did not rely on wooden materials, which eventually get weakened by time, weather, and teredo worms (also known as shipworms). With hundreds of braces supporting the posts, a 20-centimetre-thick slab of concrete 72 metres wide was pushed out 213 metres into the harbour. Surmounting this great pier went a two-storey building of solid concrete, the top floor of which was devoted to the processing of immigrants to Canada. All told, the thing would consume 70,000 tons of concrete.

If anybody was concerned about Halifax ending up with an oversupply of docking space, they needn't have been—because it didn't happen. The First World War arrived, and Halifax was inundated with convoy ships and immediately short of dock space. New dockage got put to work as soon as it came available—and sometimes before, as events would soon prove. In describing the new Pier 2, the Liberal newspaper *The Novascotian* noted slyly:

> The two outstanding features of this work which should at present be kept in mind are that it was planned, surveyed, contracted for and commenced under the Liberal Government and that it is being built in the–at the present–much maligned original Deep Water Terminal section of Halifax Harbour–that site which the present Government discards as inadequate for their terminal scheme.[43]

By springtime in 1913, fear had given way to curiosity and even optimism. Nobody was quite sure what lay in store, but most were willing to trust those with the big plans. Still, it had been eight months since Cochrane's announcement and not much had happened. The people of Halifax could be excused for being somewhat confused, but that was soon to change. Word was out that the prime minister was coming to town. Everything was about to become very clear.

⧺⧺⧺⧺⧺⧺⧺⧺

On Saturday, June 14, fifteen thousand people met the PM's train at the North Street Station, where the Macdonald Bridge and Barrington Street intersect today, deep in what had become ICR country, despite its deficiencies. The railway yard was down the hill in what is now the parking lot for HMC Dockyard.

Regally propped in a chauffeur-driven McKay automobile (built at the spanking-new Nova Scotia Carriage and Motor Car Company plant in Amherst, NS), the ride was a triumphant visit to Halifax for the prime minister. Accompanied by his trusted lieutenant, Railways and Canals Minister Frank Cochrane, Robert Laird Borden, like Julius Caesar, arrived in town to anoint the grand leap forward. Pipers puffed, buttons gleamed, chests swelled with pride as the band played "See, the Conquering Hero Comes."

The docks of the Deep Water Terminus, now believed to be in its twilight, fanned out into the harbour like fingers on an outstretched hand. There in plain sight was the partly constructed "new Pier 2," a monument to the lack of foresight of the previous Liberal government—in the opinion of the present government—with updated immigration processing facilities soon to be built and then replaced by Pier 21 at the Ocean Terminals. Nobody at that time realized how important Pier 2 would turn out to be when the First World War came to town.

In a speech at City Hall that evening, the PM was careful to reassure the unconvinced. "I believe the government can show good warrant and just cause for everything that has been proposed in regard to the terminals, and that, when the proposals are understood there will be no difference of opinion as to the wisdom of the plans."[44]

Famous last words.

The scattered Halifax railway properties that had been erected over the past half century stretched from modern-day Scotia Square, north through Richmond and Africville, up to the intersection of Young and Windsor Streets, and on to the Bedford Basin, all the while jostling for space with the dockyard and the shipyard in the constricted area between The Narrows and the steep ground below Brunswick Street, the product of "several decades of improvised, imperfect solutions," in the words of author Douglas Smith.[45]

No wonder they were replacing it. Yet there was a sizeable cadre who fought to the bitter end in their conviction that this could all be rejigged to meet the growing country's need for a large and modern East Coast port—and the new Pier 2 was evidence. (Most of it would be gone over the coming decades as the Ocean Terminals got completed and the dockyard expanded during the Second World War.)

Two weeks after Borden's visit, July 1, 1913, saw the release of a lavish hard-bound volume that Frederick Cowie prepared for Minister Cochrane. Complete with colour illustrations, it laid out the background work that had driven the decision to build in the South End and went on to provide details sure to embolden the timid and inspire the converted. It prepared the ground for the next event on July 31, the day the naysayers had dreaded. As the sun rose, *Morning Chronicle* readers met the glum headline, "Start to Cut up City Today."[46] Three sentences was all the dejected newspaper was willing to devote to the subject; the next day was no better. All they could offer then was a long, despondent editorial under the headline, "The Vandalism Begins."[47]

By the middle of August, Frederick Gutelius announced that two locomotives, along with thirty-eight dumping cars, were to arrive shortly, and two Bucyrus steam shovels were on the way from Chicago. Sharp-eyed heavy equipment enthusiasts still see older cranes carrying the moniker Bucyrus-Erie. Seventy-seven of their steam shovels were used on construction of the Panama Canal, which would be operating a year later. Being steam-powered, these machines burned coal and, like a ship or a train, had a coal bunker, furnace, water tank, boiler, and engine, and required a crew of four to operate. The shovels arrived by ship and were unloaded at the Esplanade on September 18, 1913.

The sight of those monsters allayed any fear—or desire—that the government might change its mind.

CHAPTER 9

BRINGING HEAVEN DOWN FROM ABOVE

We have got to base the development of the port of Halifax not so much upon mere local needs, as upon the wider outlook, the needs of the whole Dominion.[48]

– Prime Minister Robert Laird Borden

IN THE CONTEXT OF CANADIAN RAILROAD-BUILDING, WHICH HAS ENTAILED TENS OF THOUSANDS OF kilometres, laying the tracks for this project was insignificant: less that ten kilometres in distance, along with many times that in the shunting yards. The bulk of the work would be in creating the trench that promised to keep the invading trains out of sight. That would require a lot of blasting near people's homes. However, the trains would not all be out of sight. Today, near one of the busiest commutes into the city, on Chebucto Road, trains run not below but above the street—in this case, Quinpool Road by the Arm—looking down into the backyards of ten houses and six apartment buildings. On the other hand, as promised, nowhere along the course would a street and the track meet at a level crossing. Instead, concrete bridges kept the tracks above or below the streets, thereby keeping people, horses, cars, and trains from running into one another.

Project design was the work of Ross & Macdonald of Montréal. Two general contractors, one working on land and the other on and under the water, did the bulk of the construction. On July 4, 1913, a consortium of Cook Construction Company of Sudbury, ON, and Wheaton Brothers of Amherst, NS, was selected to do the land part.

The work was split into two sections of track. For the section between Rockingham on the basin and Jubilee Road, their winning contract came to $407,995; they contracted the second section between Jubilee Road and Reid's Rock at Point Pleasant Park for $1,035,160.

A. B. Cook was well known in railway circles, having laid a thousand or more kilometres of track for customers like the Canadian Pacific Railway (CPR) in Ontario and the National Transcontinental Railway in New Brunswick. Cook provided the heavy equipment, including steam-powered shovels, steam locomotives, and dumping cars to carry the materials from the excavation to the dump sites at the seashore. The consortium drilled and blasted the rock, built the breakwater, dug the roadbed, infilled the railway yards, laid the track, and built the bridges above the completed railway.

Going forward, I will refer to this consortium as Cook and Wheaton. Andrew Wheaton was the main contact with the customer—the federal government—and the city.

The total effort initially contracted for was to create the cut and build the railway yards and tracks up to the site of the station, the passenger landing quay (today called Piers 20, 21, and 22), Pier A, and two basins. That would provide docking for nine steamships. The design was for thirty-six steamship berths in total, with the others to be contracted at a later date. The work did not include the passenger station building, the immigration building, and the freight and passenger sheds, nor did it include the other piers that were never built but were included on maps for decades, causing confusion with the historical record.

The blasting and excavating would generate the material to fill in the harbour at each end of the line, amounting to 115 acres of land expected to be added for the railway yards, sheds, and docks. That was a lot of stone and gravel to be moved at a time when there was nothing like the powerful diesel tractors, excavators, graders, and trucks running on rubber wheels or crawler-style tracks that we see today on construction sites. Equipment moved instead on railway tracks, for which temporary rails had to be laid and removed as work locations changed. Crews would start at each end of the route and work their way to the centre while moving the rocks and gravel to the two fill sites—by rail, of course. For smaller jobs or places trains couldn't get to, trusty steeds provided the muscle.

With the contractor for the cut selected, on September 16, 1913, the Department of Railways and Canals of Canada, on behalf of Canadian Government Railways (CGR) (see chapter 17 for more on CGR), issued a tender for the first part of the dock construction. It included:

- two kilometres of quay wall,
- foundations for buildings to be constructed on the docks at a future time,
- sewers that would outflow at locations within the docks.

The specification called for forty-five feet (about fourteen metres) of depth at low tide. Add six to seven feet (two metres) to allow for high tide twice a day, plus ten feet (three metres) for the distance from the water surface to the top of the dock at high tide. That would make the quay walls some sixty-two feet (nineteen metres) high from bottom to top. It was quoted this way to ensure that there would always be a minimum of forty-five feet (fourteen metres) to float ships regardless of the tide and the height of the ship relative to the surface of the pier. That would require dredging to make the quay walls a minimum consistent depth of close to sixty-five feet (twenty metres). The digging of the railway cut by Cook and Wheaton would provide the rock and gravel for filling, as would the material from the dredging.

The two kilometres of quay wall would consist of:

- the 610-metre-long passenger landing quay,
- Pier A, 381 metres in length, and half of Pier B,
- two basins (the space between two docks): Basin No. 1, 198 metres wide, and half of Basin No. 2.

Notwithstanding F. W. Cowie's sketch in his 1913 report to Frank Cochrane showing five piers like Pier A plus a breakwater—five docks of 381 metres plus the 465-metre breakwater with docking space of 381 metres on its north side—this tender only called for the 610-metre passenger quay, where three passenger liners would tie up parallel to the shoreline, along with one pier pointing out into the harbour (Pier A) and half of a second one, which would later be labelled Pier A1—two

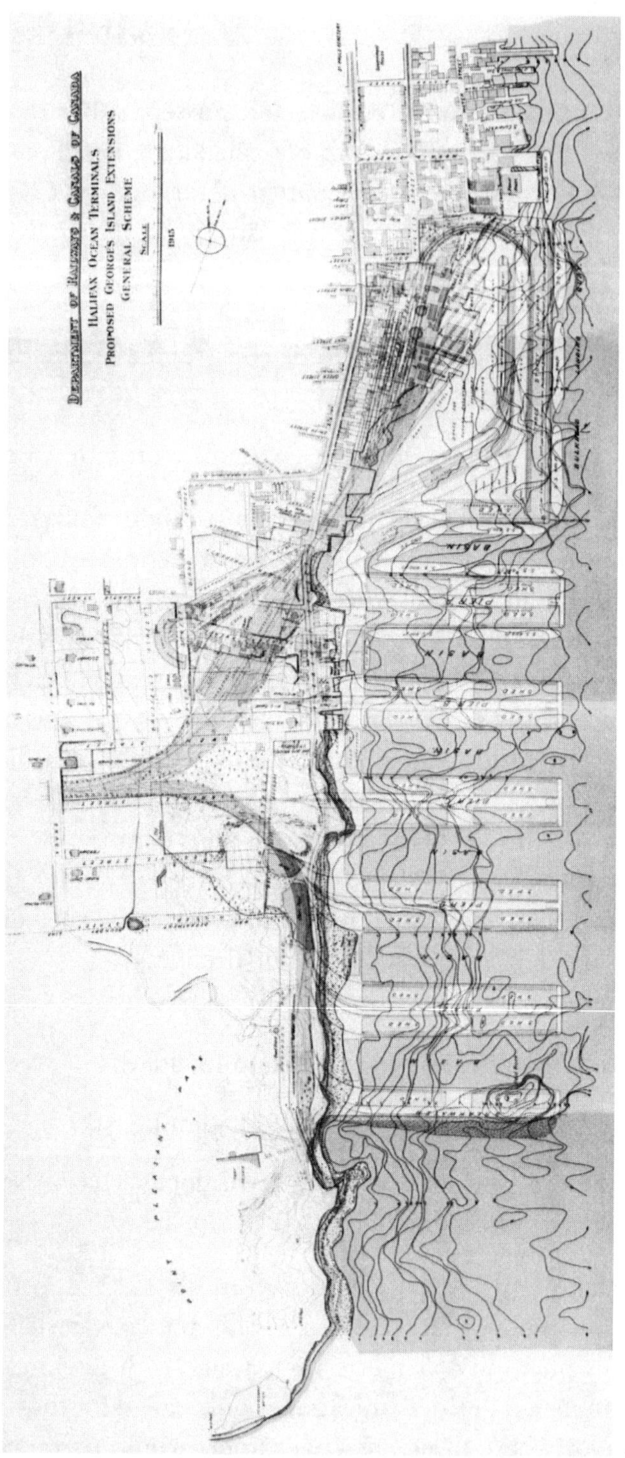

The sketch of Frederick Cowie's plan for five piers, as it appeared in his Report to the Honourable Frank Cochrane, minister of Railways and Canals, on Halifax Harbour and the development of a project of modern ocean terminals, 1913. [Canadiana Collection, Canadian Research Knowledge Network]

kilometres in all. Along with the breakwater, that was all that would be built in the first round of construction that ended in 1919—way behind schedule thanks to the war and the Halifax Explosion and the recovery period into the 1920s. After that, future progress would be affected by the Depression and the Second World War.

In November 1913 Foley, Welch, and Stewart won the tender for the dock work. Foley, Welch, and Stewart were another well-known railway construction company that had done work for railroads such as the Canadian Pacific, Canadian Northern, and Grand Trunk Pacific Railways. This job would be carried out as a joint venture with the Ottawa railroad builder Gilbert Emilius Fauquier. (The consortium, which labelled itself "Foley Bros, Welch, Stewart, and Fauquier" will be referred to here as "Foley et al."[49]) They and their subcontractors did the water work, consisting of dredging and building the quay walls under a contract valued at $5,208,743. In 2025 dollars that would be $171,555,519.

The site consisted of a two-kilometre stretch of shoreline between Georges Island and what today is the parking lot at Point Pleasant Park. For ships, docking close to the harbour entrance makes coming and going straightforward and efficient, with extraneous charges like pilotage and tug fees being kept to a minimum—something always welcome in the business world. The harbour there is a large open basin in which the biggest ships afloat can manoeuvre, anchor, and pull or be pushed by tugs into the docks. It was so formed that the harbour bottom sloped off into deep water at an easy angle, providing a good foundation on which to build the seawall with a minimum of costly deep-water work, and with a manageable amount of dredging to achieve the depth of water required.

The plan was to start at the southern boundary of the Dominion Coal and Halifax Electric Companies' properties (near the Westin Nova Scotian today) and build a solid bulkhead on nearly a north/south bearing, parallel to the channel of the harbour. It would accommodate three passenger steamships at what today are Piers 20, 21, and 22. Nowadays, they can handle just two modern—larger—cruise ships. Passengers would arrive and leave using the passenger station planned for the northern end.

Cowie's design specified that at the southern extremity of this passenger quay, and oriented at right angles to it, five additional docks would ultimately be built, each extending 381 metres out from shore. Each dock was to be 98 metres wide and 110 metres from its neighbour. That would provide space for two large freight ships to tie on each side of each dock. Then, at the southern end of the project, a new breakwater would protect the ships and docks from the volatile Atlantic Ocean. It ran out from Black Rock Beach in Point Pleasant Park.

The design called for a water depth of approximately fourteen metres at low tide. To achieve that would require dredging the bottom in some places and building it up in others. Some spots would need significant infilling to get to the ideal bedrock depth of at least fourteen metres. There, concrete pedestals placed on the bedrock would form the base on which to build the wall.

Leading the dock engineering for Foley et al. was Arthur Charles Brown, a graduate of Hartley University College in Southampton, England. At twenty-four years of age, he joined the project in June 1912 as the chief assistant to the superintending engineer for CGR, James McGregor. When work on the docks got going in February 1914, Brown was promoted to resident engineer of dock construction, where he would distinguish himself as a competent and well-liked manager. An accomplished soccer player, he often played at the Wanderers Grounds in Halifax and got married during his stay in Canada, becoming the father of two Canadian daughters.

McGregor and nine engineering staff were located on-site in Miss Jessie Simson's expropriated house at 137 Pleasant Street, near the harbour.

By March 1914 a representative of Foley et al. had arranged to take possession of a building south of Inglis Street that had once been McDougall's Distillery. The interior was being rebuilt as a bunkhouse for men who would be employed on construction of the docks. Plans were under way for a kitchen and men's quarters with hot and cold running water—not bad for a bunch of navvies (migrant railway-building labourers) in 1914 and certainly better than accommodations for Cook and Wheaton employees. The Board of Control got wind that they were converting a barn for their workers to live in and promptly told them they were breaking the law.

⌗⌗⌗⌗⌗⌗⌗⌗⌗⌗⌗⌗⌗⌗⌗⌗

Four groups were interacting on the building of the railway line and docks. The first was the customer: the Government of Canada, on behalf of Canadian Government Railways, usually referred to as the Intercolonial Railway but sometimes, and less often, as the Ocean Terminals Railway. By the time the rails were laid, it would be Canadian National Railways (CNR). The second was the contractors: Cook and Wheaton and Foley et al. Cook and Wheaton loosened the ground by blasting rock, digging out the broken rock and gravel, loading it onto railway cars, transporting it to the shoreline, and dumping it into the water for Foley et al. to use in building the docks, all the while minimizing inconvenience to the people living around and sometimes among them. The third was the people who were either leaving their houses and moving to another location or having their houses moved elsewhere. In the meantime, they came and went—to work, to school, to church, to shop, to visit, by walking, driving an automobile, driving in a carriage, or riding in a tram. And finally, there was the city government that was representing the citizens and attempting to look after their interests. Their job was to make the city tick. They had lots of experience in dealing with companies that built roads and bridges, as Cook and Wheaton were doing. Their handicap was that they did not control the money as they did on city-funded public works projects—where they also selected the contractors—so their authority was fuzzy; to the contractors and the railway they were a nuisance. But to the hapless citizens, the city was where they went to complain.

CHAPTER 10

BRINGING HELL UP FROM BELOW

There were 9 tons of dynamite used in the blast, enough to destroy a great part of Halifax if used on the surface, but it was placed in holes 30 feet deep. The result was a tremendous upheaval of about 30,000 yards of rock, estimated at about 50,000 tons.[50]

– *Halifax Herald*

THE PROJECT BEGAN WITH DRILLING, BLASTING, DIGGING, DREDGING, TRANSPORTING, DUMPING, MIXING, burning, fabricating, and excavating—but mostly disrupting. For the contractors, everything started with and depended on detonating dynamite. Stone and gravel were needed to infill at the Fairview site, to infill at the Georges Island site, to ballast the tracks, and to construct the breakwater. The rate at which Foley et al. could build the underwater walls depended directly on the rate at which Cook and Wheaton dumped stone and gravel from the cut into the ocean. With a July 1, 1915, deadline to complete the job, Cook and Wheaton were under constant pressure to produce.

For the residents, it was the beginning of a nightmare. Those who lost their homes and had to move were greatly aggrieved, but those who had to live nearby, whom we may call the lesser aggrieved, did not fare well either. At any given time, somebody was being forced to tolerate deafening noise, water in the basement, thick coal smoke in the air, debris flying above, the ground shaking below, laundry covered in soot, the water cut off, or obstacles blocking the way to their homes.

Above: A steam shovel loading debris from the rail cut onto hopper cars, ca. 1916. When loaded, the train backed up to deliver the stone to the shoreline for use as fill. Photo was taken from the footbridge crossing the cut at Young Avenue. The large houses in the upper left background belonged to Hugh Silver and Samuel Brookfield. [HALIFAX MUNICIPAL ARCHIVES, MACLAUCHLAN PHOTO (CR6-122.30)] *Below: Rubble being removed from another point along the rail cut.* [TOM LYNSKEY COLLECTION]

Then there were the chronically aggrieved, which ironically included the booster-in-chief, Michael Dwyer, and the city engineer, FWW Doane. Young Avenue, where they lived, along with Tower Road, suffered the widest, deepest gash and spanned the area with the most intense disruption for the longest time, enduring the most blasting and the most excavating, rounded out by construction of the two most complex, highest, and longest bridges.

Their homes were within sight of the main construction site, where endless drilling, blasting, and digging took place. Every movement of any piece of equipment working on the trench rattled past their doors. The incessant coal smoke from the steam engines driving the drills, shovels, trains, crushers, conveyors, mixers, barges, and tugs was their constant companion.

This was not to be a short-lived inconvenience for days, weeks, or months. It went on for years. The first steam engine started clanking in 1913. When the work reached Young Avenue, the residents, to get anywhere in the city, had to detour around the end of the trench that was being excavated. As the trench moved past and continued to lengthen, so did the detour. In the summer of 1914, a year after construction began, the contractors erected a footbridge across the cut. It remained there until they completed the permanent bridge at the beginning of 1918.

Now, after more than a century of use, some of these bridges have been replaced and the rest are in need of replacement. Each requires at least a year of work. Not only do people have to live with the noise of the freight trains winding through their otherwise peaceful neighbourhoods, but they also have to live for a year or more with the inconvenience of not being able to drive to their homes because the neighbourhood bridge is the only way over the deep, wide cut—and they have to use a footbridge.

Incredibly, there had been little to no collaboration or planning with the city, either from the federal government or the railway company.[51] That changed somewhat when they got into the details of things like bridges, routing changes, moving buildings, and site security, and only because the city engineer stayed on top of things. He had to; his home depended on it.

Work started at the Fairview end of the rail line and about a month later at the Georges Island end. By April 1914 work at the Georges Island end had progressed to Tower Road while crews at the other end were working between Bayers Road and Mumford Road. For digging, the contractors eventually employed five steam shovels consisting of two 100-ton, two 60-ton, and one 70-ton shovel, along with a 20-ton standard-gauge locomotive crane that ran on railway tracks. This was before the days of the crawler-type tracks common on modern bulldozers and excavators. Digging their way through the rough terrain down in the railway cut required careful planning to ensure that minimal time was consumed in laying, taking up, and moving temporary railway track so the shovels could change location.

Two steam shovels work among five sets of temporary tracks near the basin with the Bayers Road temporary footbridge in the background. [TOM LYNSKEY COLLECTION]

Much of what needed excavating in the railway cut was shale rock that had to be drilled and blasted. The drilling was complicated by the seams within the rock containing sand and gravel that fell down into the holes after the drill was removed. It took some trial and error, but the drilling crews finally settled on a six-inch diameter drill inside a case pipe, a bit like drilling a well. With this, they bored two metres below where the railway bed would be located, inserted the dynamite charge and "fired a shot"—jargon for blasting. In areas where they had to go more than ten metres deep, a second bore was required.

The blasting would become the biggest ordeal for those living near the site. For three years, there was ongoing friction between the contractors and people who lived along the route. While one group was trying to get a court injunction to stop the blasting, another was petitioning City Hall to do something, another was trying to get compensation for damages, and yet another group of thrill seekers was trying to get nearer the action—to the great annoyance of the contractors. Especially irksome for others was the use of "coyote holes." These were tunnels excavated at the bottom of the rock face and packed with explosives which, when detonated, caused an unusually potent explosion which, of course, produced an especially fruitful yield of broken stone. The problem was that they caused a lot of noise and vibration that only enhanced the fears of those living nearby.

The contractors estimated that they blasted out 1.5 million cubic metres of rock that went to the shorelines at the two sites in sixteen-cubic-metre side-dumping railway cars where it got dumped overboard. By mid-1916, twenty-two acres of land had been reclaimed at the shoreline that stretched from across from Georges Island to Point Pleasant. The material from the western end of the cut was dumped into the Bedford Basin between Rockingham and Fairview. On top of it they constructed a freight yard that could accommodate 1,540 railway cars and is still in use. Why so much space? Because even though a train speeding along the tracks looks sleek and free-flowing, it takes a lot of shuttling and switching of tracks to store, sort, classify, order, load, unload, repair, and clean the cars and assemble each train.

Crews of navvies were kept busy building and rebuilding tracks for the heavy equipment. A trainload of rocks and gravel would arrive on

Building the breakwater. McNabs Island is in the background. Barely visible on the far right is the Maugher Beach lighthouse. [Tom Lynskey collection]

the track that ran along the shoreline. The cars would get dumped and the materials were levelled with a plough, called a leveller, attached to the side of the locomotive. When the rock was smoothed out, the track was moved closer to the shore while the train went for the next load.

Though that was trying and tedious, building the breakwater out from where the lower parking lot is now located at Point Pleasant Park was worse. It ran from shore at right angles, jutting a shade under 475 metres—almost half a kilometre—out toward the shipping channel. Being a breakwater, it was by definition erected at a location where rough and destructive weather could be expected. Cook and Wheaton got started in June 1914 when they built a temporary wooden trestle—like a wharf—about 90 metres out from shore, over which the railway cars loaded with stone were pushed and then dumped.[52] Then they moved the operation onto the top of what they had completed, covering it with track and pushing the carloads of stone out over the water on a steel span 12 metres long, supported at its outer end by a 27-metre-long barge and at the inner end by the breakwater itself. The tides complicated the process, causing the barge to move up and down while the inner end remained static. To compensate for this, they had to constantly pump and remove water from the barge to keep it level with the inner end.

When completed, the breakwater's 10-metre width consisted of rock from the railway cutting protected on the outside with heavy stone slabs five to eight tons in weight. Its outer tip would eventually anchor the second steel anti-submarine net that guarded the entrance to the harbour during the First World War, running across to Ives Point on McNabs Island. The first net, deployed in 1915, stretched from downtown to Georges Island and then across to the Dartmouth shore near Eastern Passage. The second one, deployed in late 1916, ran from Ives Point to the breakwater. The net deployed during the Second World War was farther out, past Maugher Beach.

Cowie's long-term plan for the breakwater was that the surface would be sheeted over with concrete or wooden planks and the inner side would be configured for tying up freighters. That never came to pass.

CHAPTER 11

THE CHICKENS COME HOME TO ROOST

As the location of the Ocean Terminals has depreciated the value of property along Young Avenue, we feel that the city should do anything within its power to help to offset this loss.[53]

– W. A. Black and Michael Dwyer

STAND UPON THE YOUNG AVENUE BRIDGE THAT TAKES CARS AND PEDESTRIANS ACROSS THE NINETY-METRE gap to Point Pleasant Park and you immediately get in tune with its violent past. Gaze out toward the harbour and you realize you're standing where the rock cut begins to widen into a vast area of flat ground covered in railway tracks. The ground is level because much of it has been infilled with the product of all the blasting and digging. What you are beholding was once gently sloping fields, streets, houses, shoreline, and then the water of the harbour lapping the seashore. Today it is as flat as a tabletop and just as hard, where once it was alive and inviting.

You are standing on what was the longest bridge in metro Halifax before the Angus L. Macdonald Bridge crossed the harbour in 1955. You are fifteen metres above the tracks that run in from the Bedford Basin at Fairview Cove. The cliffs along the railway cut are taller here than anywhere else along the route. The original cut was equipped with double tracks but it's cheaper to run fewer, longer trains, so one track suffices now. Below you, that track has morphed into six and continues to the water as it replicates into dozens that progress to the container terminal piers, the Ocean Terminals Berths, the passenger station, and the yards where the trains, often hundreds of cars long, get assembled for their journeys into the centre of the North American continent.

In 1918, to rationalize the Canadian railway network of money-losing companies, the Canadian government formed the CNR, which proceeded to acquire the ICR, Canadian Northern, National Transcontinental, and Grand Trunk Pacific Railways, themselves consolidations of dozens of smaller railroads. It still operates across Canada to Vancouver and south to the Gulf of Mexico. With 31,000 kilometres of track, the now-privatized CN Rail is Canada's biggest and the only railroad in North America to terminate on three coasts. A big chunk of its business originates with those tracks you're looking down on.

Young Avenue was the first street that was cut in two to accommodate the railroad, and its residents were the first to get a taste of what lay ahead. The project's chief booster, Michael Dwyer, lived at 11 Young Avenue, near the southernmost end of the street. What he was living through was not what he thought he had signed on for. A year and a half after leading the ecstatic Board of Trade chorale in a round of "For He's a Jolly Good Fellow," he was giving the Board of Control an earful. Along with shipowner William A. Black and others from Young Avenue, he was trying to convince them to build a concrete sidewalk along his street. The area normally went through a muddy period in spring but, with the construction this year, it was turning into a quagmire for the city to fix, not the railway! In addition, the air was cracking and his house was quaking from the dynamite, his water was about to be cut off, he didn't know how he was going to get across the gap in the road, and he feared the daunting prospect of having to ease his bare bottom over the unwelcoming hole of an outdoor privy while they figured out how to replace the Young Avenue sewage service that was soon to disappear. James McGregor planned to send the effluent into a tank, which would be periodically dumped into Steele's (also sometimes spelled Steel's) Pond near Point Pleasant Park. FWW didn't think much of that idea. The city told McGregor to send it instead into a brook that crossed railway property into the harbour, a more characteristic solution for the time. Steele's Pond, prominent in tales of old Halifax, was lost in 1952 during the building of the Seaward Defence Base.

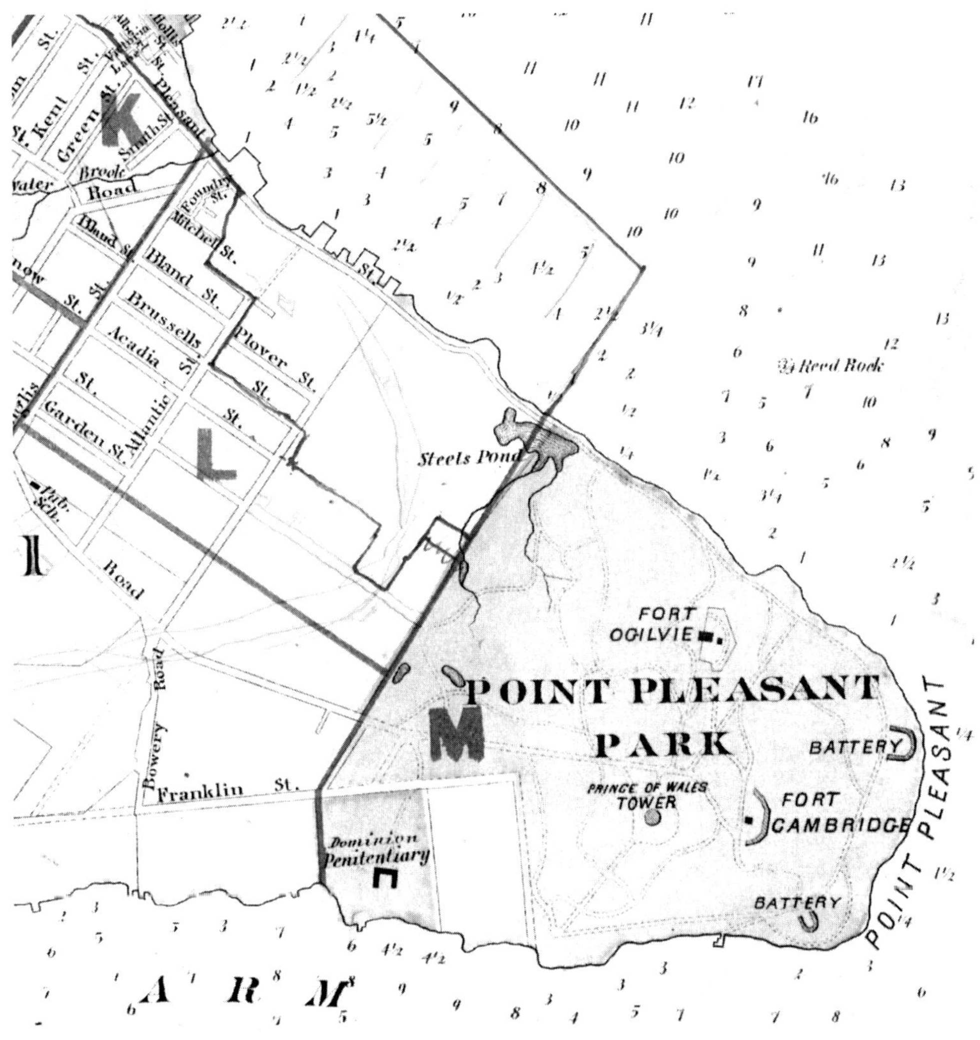

A portion of an 1878 Hopkins City Atlas map of Halifax showing the location of Steele's Pond. William Roue, the designer of Canada's famous racing schooner Bluenose, *used to sail models of his designs in Steele's Pond to test their performance.* [H. W. HOPKINS NS ARCHIVES LIBRARY O/S G 1129 H3 H67 1878]

Residents on Plover Street have complained to the city officials about the condition of the sewer, it having been cut off during the progress of the work on the ocean terminals. The matter was referred to the City Engineer and in a report he states that it is proposed to carry the Atlantic Street sewer east to the diversion of the fresh water brook sewer. Until that is completed there is no outlet for the Plover Street sewer. The number of houses discharging through this latter is comparatively small, and there is such a large flow of surface and ground water compared to the amount of sewage that the latter is very much diluted before reaching the railway cutting.[116] – *Halifax Herald*, September 28, 1916.

Why did the city's most influential people permit such carnage, even to their own properties? The Board of Trade and the majority of the city's titans of commerce had felt they had to accept Cochrane's plan as presented, fearing that if they did not it would open the door for the naysayers to barge in and spoil everything. As Murray Hodgins wrote, "For the project's Halifax supporters, the goal was simply to secure federal money for the port as soon as possible, no matter what the cost. The public was manipulated into accepting the location by the government's use of optimistic projections for economic growth and by its refusal to allow the city a role in the planning process."[54]

Look down from the bridge while glancing left and right and you are met with ugly brown jagged cliffs that tell a long and cacophonous story of drilling and blasting, day after day, month after month. Houses line the tops of these cliffs, most built after a modicum of silence had been restored. The incessant explosions were replaced with clank, clank, clickety clack. The sound of idling diesel locomotives is what passes now for quiet, where track after track is filled with railway cars full of shipping containers holding everything we need and plenty of things we do not.

Navvies building the final Young Avenue bridge in November 1917. Louisa Smith's and John MacInnes's houses can be seen in the background. [Halifax Municipal Archives CR6-122.462]

The project was barely rolling when FWW, who was not a member of the Board of Trade, had become concerned about how the contractor was doing things. Having become the city engineer in 1891 at the age of twenty-eight, he had at this point been in the job for twenty-two years and was well regarded. On November 10, 1913, he expressed his alarm in a report to Mayor Bligh.

> For some time, I have noticed that the contractor of the Terminal Railway is using heavy charges in blasting. He is drilling deep holes, and throwing out very large boulders, throwing large pieces of rock for some distance.
>
> The work as carried on is a menace to everybody living in the neighbourhood and if the whole work is to be carried on in this manner, it will be very dangerous at street crossings.

> The contractor has built a structure, which I am informed is a dynamite magazine, about 50 yards from a house on Young Avenue and about 75 yards from another house. When the excavation approaches Young Avenue, if he continues to use the same heavy charges, the situation will be a serious one and I do not think he should be permitted to store dynamite so near the blasting. The district is solid rock and such heavy blasting may cause serious, if not fatal, accidents."[55]

Andrew Wheaton, one of the two Wheaton Brothers who shared the contract with Cook Construction, blamed the onlookers for being too inquisitive. In a letter to the mayor, he observed: "Numbers of citizens are accustomed to visit the places where we are at work to stand watching the operations. When we are ready to set off blasts we at times find great difficulty in getting the onlookers to retire to places of safety."[56]

He decided to ask the mayor if he had any ideas and suggested that perhaps, "such of your police force as may be available to warn citizens" might be used to keep people from standing too close. More than two years of blasting remained and the best he could come up with to ensure the safety of the curious was to look for ideas from the mayor and maybe borrow a few police officers when they weren't busy.

When they had quoted the job, the contractors knew they would be working in the middle of the city, and they should have realized the peculiar nature of the work. They would be slicing through the city, creating a deep, impassable cleft that would separate neighbours—and they would be at it for years. This was the biggest project the people of Halifax had ever seen, and it was happening in their midst—in fact, in some people's front yards. Of course they were going to be curious. No doubt it was a favourite Sunday afternoon outing to take the tram across town to gawk at the destruction and wonder if their city could ever be put back together again.

Even though this project was not of the mayor's making, the problems fell to him anyway. When peace in the neighbourhood is disturbed, who gets the call? City Hall! By November 5, 1913, Mayor Bligh had received so many complaints about the blasting that he ordered the city engineer to look into it and send him a report.

The last thing FWW needed was more work, but he was powerless to avoid being drawn into the huge undertaking. He was also not the type to just stand by, especially when his own house was being threatened. Like the mayor, he would have been happy not having to deal with problems caused by the contractors who were working, not for the city, but for the federal government. The city works department was swamped with routine work and complaints were flooding into the Board of Control about delays with various areas that called for FWW's engineers, while his bosses were leaning on him to come up with a solution.[57]

To begin his investigation, he consulted the city solicitor, F. H. Bell, an opponent of the Ocean Terminals project who feared it would drive up property taxes by as much as 3 percent. Bell met with the contractors. Meanwhile, the city engineer was getting complaints that the contractors were taking copious amounts of city water from the fire hydrants without paying for it.

By January 16, C. Ochiltree Macdonald, of 35 Young Avenue—FWW's next-door neighbour—had to let off some steam. He fired off a letter to the mayor complaining about the unsafe way in which the contractors were handling the blasting (see sidebar on page 91). That initiated a letter from the city clerk to Andrew Wheaton, asking him to appear at the next meeting of the Board of Control. He didn't show. Another letter followed promptly, which incited him to turn up on January 26, 1914, accompanied by H. F. McLean, the contractor's project manager. Predictably, Wheaton felt Macdonald was exaggerating the danger to his household. In response, FWW, who lived between Michael Dwyer and Macdonald, produced a large rock that had supposedly landed in the yard of another Young Avenue resident, suggesting it would be safer if the contractors blasted earlier in the day when there were fewer pedestrians around. But there was more to it than that. Multiple blasts were being ignited simultaneously, often from a depth of ten metres, in a line thirty and sixty metres across the cut. Macdonald wanted them to use smaller charges, but that would have messed up the engineering of the blasts and would have been more costly for the contractors.

> Sir: The blasting carried on by the Cook Construction Co. and Wheaton Brothers eastward of Young Avenue is becoming a source of pressing danger to my premises and family. About 4:00 P.M. today a blast set off at or near the intersection of Owen and Plover Streets hurled rock so far that it fell into my garden at a part usually frequented by members of my family. I am informed by a person in the upper part of my house [that rocks] fell onto my roof and still more onto Young Avenue. I have secured the stone first referred to which Mrs. Macdonald and the writer saw fall upon the premises. It had travelled about 550 feet. As my house is, in one place, only about 60 feet from the "right of way" the danger must increase if that description of blasting is carried on....
>
> I beg to make formal application for civic protection and trust that the authority of the city be exerted to prevent injury to my family or property by this dangerous system of explosions. Yours truly, C. Ochiltree Macdonald.

McLean insisted that they took every precaution in alerting the public, posting workers on each street in affected areas to give warning of upcoming blasts. And, not surprisingly, when asked about the water poaching, Wheaton declared it was his understanding that they were paying for any city water they used. The city had already decreed that contractors would have to pay for water just like everybody else. On August 6, 1913, just days after the project got started, the city advised them that metered pipes would be provided at the point of need and they would be charged for usage based on the meter data.

It was proposed that controller Charles Hoben and FWW make a site visit from which they could come up with recommendations regarding the blasting. FWW, however, suggested there was no point in the two of them making a visit because he and Hoben disagreed on how to solve the problem. He noted that the controller was a friend of Andrew Wheaton so—well, you know. Hoben challenged FWW as to what he was insinuating and called on Wheaton for support. The latter declared that he had never gotten a favour from Hoben and had never asked for one.[58]

Tensions rose. Word about the tiff soon made it to the street. Then Hoben derailed the next board meeting when he presented a letter:

> Herewith I hand you clippings from "The Halifax Herald" and "The Morning Chronicle" of this date, of a report of a meeting of the Board of Control held on the 26th. It will be seen that reference has been made in these papers to remarks of the City Engineer concerning myself and my civic relations with the Cook Construction Co., Limited & Wheaton Bros. These remarks of the City Engineer before the Board of Control, published in the press of the City, constitute a very serious reflection upon my civic integrity and are calculated to damage my usefulness as a Controller and do me injury.
>
> I cannot allow the public statement of the City Engineer that "Mr. Wheaton is a friend of mine and that I favour his company in every way I can" along with other insinuations to go unnoticed.[59]

Hoben was the controller of the Works Department, which meant he was the city's main contact for the project. It was crucial that he be seen to be squeaky clean. Instead, he was in the papers under circumstances that politicians deplore—and he was at loggerheads with an important senior member of city staff.

With a full agenda, the board now had to deal with a formal request from one of its members asking to be relieved of the administration of the Works Department while the investigation progressed, and committing to resign from the Board of Control, "if a shadow of collusion or civic favouritism is disclosed reflecting upon myself in the administration of my department towards the Cook Construction Company & Wheaton Brothers or any other company."[60]

The spotlight focussed menacingly on FWW. Under questioning from his bosses, he stated that he did not intend any remarks he might have made at the meeting on the 26th as a charge against Controller Hoben, but to show the board that having him and Hoben visit the construction site would not be productive. After some clarification, Controller O'Connor put forward a motion for FWW to express to the board if he thought Controller Hoben would allow himself to be influenced by the friendship of any citizen or contractor in dealing with civic matters. The motion was seconded and read to FWW. Swallowing hard, no doubt, he replied that he had no intention of making any such imputation against Controller Hoben.

With that blowup defused, it was back to the matter of how the contractor was handling the blasting. Robert Daw, an observer at the meeting, suggested that the city engage an expert in blasting work for a few days to investigate the operations and report to the engineer. That matter was referred to none other than Controller Hoben and FWW to handle.

As for the water the contractors were helping themselves to, that had to be deferred to another meeting. In the meantime, Ewan Morrison, superintendent of the water department, was instructed to investigate a claim that somebody in the department had told somebody at Cook and Wheaton that they could use city water free of charge. Morrison reported back that he had questioned every employee of the department and, as he no doubt anticipated, nobody had any knowledge of such a claim.

On February 23, 1914, the matter was again before the Board of Control. With very little discussion, there was a motion on the floor to prosecute Cook and Wheaton for unlawfully taking water from the city water service without permission. It was promptly seconded. After further discussion with the city solicitor and FWW, the controllers relented, deciding to instruct the company to caution their employees not to take water without permission and that, upon a recurrence, they would indeed be prosecuted.

On February 25, FWW updated the mayor:

> As far as I can see, no steps have been taken to avoid damage, except that C. O. Mcdonald's [*sic*] house has been boarded up. A few days ago, a blast threw a heavy rock or lump of frozen earth through the roof of Alfred Whitman's house, over two hundred yards away, and at the same time, smaller pieces fell around William Robertson and Rev. James Falconer, who were walking along the street. Yesterday, the noon blast cut off the water entirely from Young Avenue, and the houses on that street have been without it ever since.[61]

Macdonald's house was actually boarded up in preparation for being moved across Owen Street and farther along Young Avenue, away from the cut. The house of his neighbour, Louisa Smith, was also moved across Owen as it was too close to the route the cut was taking.

Two days later, on February 27, the Board of Control instructed the city solicitor to procure an order from the courts restraining the contractors from carrying on blasting operations in the manner they had been doing. That motivated the contractor to start using heavy mats to keep things from flying through the air, but it did not stop the destruction. Captain John Hicks, about half a kilometre away at The Oaks, reported to FWW that a blast on March 4 was the heaviest yet and Burchell reported that it shook his house violently, destroying a quantity of china.

In their exasperating quest for solutions, the controllers decided to hire an inspector to keep an eye on the company and to make Cook and Wheaton pay the cost. In April they even received an application for the job from one J. DeWolfe of Bridgewater. Given that this person lived 100 kilometres from Halifax and no such job had been advertised, it would appear he got wind from somebody on the inside that there might be a job opportunity in the offing.

The problem lay with Cook and Wheaton alone because Foley et al. did all their blasting underwater, as they were quick to point out. Regardless, on August 10, the city clerk tried the soft sell and wrote to both contractors:

> Numerous complaints have been made to the Board of Control by citizens living within the zone of the operations being carried on in connection with construction work for the Ocean Terminals as to the manner in which the work is being prosecuted.
>
> Notwithstanding the fact that claims for property damage have been promptly met, the people in the vicinity of the works claim a substantial grievance in being warned to leave their homes when blasts are about to be set off.
>
> The Board has been advised that employees of the construction companies have not always hitherto obeyed instructions for the

> proper safeguarding of life and property from flying fragments of rock. The Board therefore desires to suggest that you will for your own protection and the relief of citizens from anxiety pay for the services of a qualified inspector to be appointed by the City to supervise protection during blasting operations.[62]

That went nowhere. Acting city solicitor R. T. MacIlreith then told the city that trying to force the contractors to pay would not fly either. There was no provision in the city charter dealing with blasting inside the city limits and council had no authority to appoint an inspector and compel the contractor to pay his salary. The blasting law was limited to one paragraph and stated:

> Every person who blasts rock with gun powder, dynamite or other explosive in any place within 100 feet from any street, highway or thoroughfare shall use the most careful precaution in giving notice thereof by blowing horns or otherwise, previous to each explosion, and shall not explode more than three bores at one time, and shall cover the spot about to be blasted, with a sufficient quantity of bushes, timber, earth, stones or other materials, to deaden the force of the explosion.[63]

Covering a blast with bushes sounds like a good way to shower the neighbourhood with greenery, but it's an ineffective way to protect the neighbours from danger. Stones sound even worse. No wonder they were raining down from on high!

With a solution to the blasting issue still evading the city fathers, the residents of Dutch Village banded together in the middle of June and presented them with a petition about the blasting in their neighbourhood near the Fairview site.

Then it got really complicated.

Haligonians learned on August 4, 1914, that Canada was at war. Before the city had time to consider what that would mean for Halifax, it received a list of city employees deemed to be significant to the war effort. The talented and energetic leader of the engineering department, FWW Doane, was on the list. Having been an officer in the militia for more than a dozen years, he put his name on the active service roster on August 11. He could be called up at any time. He and his wife, Alice, had two sons, William—Billie—and Harvey, of the right age, so Alice had a lot to worry about.

In the meantime, lawyer Fred Pearson decided to take action, and came looking to the mayor for support.

> Recently great blasts have been set off near Franklyn Street. Serious injury to surrounding properties has occurred and various people have run great risk of serious injury to themselves, and I have determined not to wait until someone is killed or badly hurt, and I have commenced an action in the name of the Attorney General in order that it may be decided that people should not have to go hourly in risk of their lives.[64]

A year later, the letters were still coming in. In an address to the Union of Nova Scotia Municipalities on August 23, 1916, the engineer in charge of dock construction, Arthur Brown, made this comment:

> The contractors prosecuted their work with great energy and it speaks well for the care they exercised that in drilling and shooting [blasting] over 1½ million cubic yards of rock very little damage was done to property and there were no serious accidents to the workmen.[65]

That may have been true at the time, but less than two months later, there was an accident that took a life. At 4:00 A.M. on the morning of October 18, Daniel McDonald climbed inside a crane that was working on the quay wall. The fireman and engineer had been outside, and he had stepped inside to warm up when the ground beneath gave way and the crane slid into the water with McDonald inside. The company's divers extricated his body.[66]

It's interesting that Brown chose to highlight the low injury record to the "workmen." Compare that to this notation from the Board of Control minutes for August 30, 1915:

> Read letter S. R. Cossey, stating that in consequence of the conditions in which the Ocean Terminals Contractors had left Jubilee Road, his wife had received severe injuries, and that if her health is seriously affected or she should lose her life as a result, he will hold the City responsible.

More than three years after the project began, rocks were still flying through the air. On November 10, 1916, a forty-pounder went through the roof of the boathouse of the Northwest Arm Rowing Club at the foot of South Street, damaging two boats and two canoes.

Municipal officials were in an impossible situation.

CHAPTER 12

WHO YOU GONNA CALL?

We went to a great deal of expense on this contract to inconvenience the people as little as possible but we know there must be some little inconvenience at times, which is unavoidable, and if the people will bear with this patiently for another three or four months we think the cause for complaints will all be over, and we will assure them, in the meantime, that we will cause as little trouble as possible.[67]

– Andrew Wheaton, Contractor

AS THE CREWS DUG THEIR WAY ACROSS THE CITY, THEY TORE THROUGH ROADS, SIDEWALKS, BACKYARDS, walking trails, water lines, and sewer pipes. In April 1915 the blasting stopped up the outlet for the South Bland Street sewer. The next day there was a rainstorm and every house along the street was flooded, some with their basements full of foul water up to the ceiling.

Bridges were needed to cross the railway cuttings at Young Avenue, Tower Road, and Bower Road—the area with the deepest and most complex cuts. People on the wrong sides found themselves removed from the rest of the city while the contractors designed and built temporary bridges for them to cross the gaps.

Needless to say, the bridges were essential to their lives. In April 1914 the Board of Control became concerned about the inability of firefighting equipment to get across the breach at Young Avenue and Tower Road. The city solicitor advised the contractors that the city could invoke conditions of the federal Government Railways Act to force the contractors to build robust temporary bridges connecting the south side of the cut with the rest of the city.

Letters flew back and forth between the railway, the contractors, the city, and the citizens. Most of these interchanges took place between FWW, the senior engineer for the city, and James McGregor, the senior engineer for the railway, as they banged their heads together. This particular exchange begins with FWW's response to a plan McGregor had proposed three days earlier for a bridge across the gap at Young Avenue.[68]

Note to readers: Spellings and punctuation in this section are consistent with the original letters.

January 8, 1915

From: FWW Doane, City Engineer

To: James McGregor, Superintending Engineer of Canadian Government Railways

In reply to your letter of 5th inst. [meaning the 5th of the current month, i.e. January 5] respecting a proposed foot bridge near Young Avenue to accommodate the public, I shall submit the plan to the Board of Control at its next meeting.

I regret that you are not making provision for carrying the water pipe across the cutting at this point, as the absence of a direct water supply at this point effects the fire service and the erection of a foot bridge instead of a traffic bridge for vehicles makes fire protection service much more difficult. Your proposal may not meet with the approval of the Board of Control. It will, of course, be a great improvement on the present inconvenient, dangerous and unsatisfactory crossing which pedestrians have to use now to get to that portion of Young Avenue below the railway.

July 21, 1915

From: James McGregor, Superintending Engineer

To: Fred Monaghan, Halifax City Clerk

The matter of temporary crossings, diversions, and bridges for the existing roads and streets crossing the right-of-way of the Halifax Ocean Terminals Ry. [Railway] is receiving my careful attention and it is our intention to continue as heretofore to make suitable arrangements for these crossings to meet the public convenience as far as is practicable.

Before receiving your letter I had taken the matter up in detail with the Contractors and I feel confident that the arrangements that we have made and will carry out will be satisfactory to the Board of Control and the public generally.

August 6, 1915

From: Fred Pearson, Lawyer and citizen

To: Mayor Peter Martin

On several occasions during the past week the bridge over the railway cutting on Bower Road has been closed, and in the event of a fire on Francklyn Street, Tower Road or Young Avenue, the fire apparatus might have been altogether prevented from, or greatly delayed in reaching the scene. I beg to direct your attention to the present condition of the bridge and to ask you to be good enough to have such inspection made as will indicate as to whether or not the fire apparatus could get safely over the bridge even now. This is a matter of vital importance to the residents living south of the railway ditch, and I should be very much gratified if you would kindly direct the proper department to give the matter early attention.

August 14, 1915

From: Fred Pearson, Lawyer

To: Mayor Peter Martin

At various times since the work on the terminal railways started, I have found it necessary to direct the attention of the Superintending Engineer to the fact that very little, if any, attention was paid to the convenience of the public. I have particular reference to road diversions, temporary bridges and the approaches thereto. On August 12, I received a letter from James McGregor, Superintending Engineer, in which the following paragraph appears:

"In the whole matter of temporary roads, bridges and crossings the convenience and rights of the general public have never been lost sight of by me. In all our arrangements, we are endeavouring to carry out our works to the satisfaction of the Board of Control and City Council as the responsible representatives of the public."

I desire to draw the attention of the Board of Control to the fact that no road diversions for the passage of vehicular traffic have been constructed to take care of the traffic on Young Avenue since the ditch was built. The same is true with respect to Tower Road. I would also direct your attention to the approach to the bridge on Bower Road and to the method of carrying the water pipes across that bridge. I might also point out that the lighting of the bridge at night is entirely unsatisfactory.

During the past week, the Superintending Engineer had ordered gravel to be placed on the approaches and unless some proper binding material is placed on top of the gravel, the cure will be worse than the disease.

I am directing these matters to your attention because Mr. McGregor informs me that he is carrying out this work to your satisfaction, and I am not inclined to believe that this is the case. If it is, I should be very glad indeed to learn from you what instructions, if any, have been given as the method of carrying on the work.

My remarks, of course, only apply to that part of the terminal railway between Bower Road and the water front, but I understand generally that the same policy of ignoring public convenience is followed in other sections of the city.

I am informed that it is not the intention of the Superintending Engineer to place permanent bridges on Young Avenue, Tower Road and Bower Road, but that one or two bridges are to be constructed to serve these three arteries of travel. I am further informed that the bridge proposed for Young Avenue is only designed to be about half the width of the roadway and sidewalks. I think this is a matter which should engage the attention of the Board of Control.

August 18, 1915

From: Fred Monaghan, City Clerk

To: Board of Control Minutes

Read letter G. Fred Pearson complaining of methods employed by contractors in carrying out their work, they apparently disregarding the City's interests entirely in same. Reference was also made to proposed bridges, it being pointed out that they understood it was the intention not to erect same in accordance with original plans.

Referred to the City Engineer with the request that a detailed report be made on the several points taken up in same.

August 20, 1915

From: James McGregor, Superintending Engineer

To: FWW Doane, City Engineer

I beg to state that I am having the temporary roads and road diversions at Bower Road and Clarence Street surfaced with fine gravel.

To consolidate this gravel and get smooth hard surfaces as soon as possible, I shall be glad to know if the city will cooperate with us to the extent of having these roads thoroughly rolled with their steam roller.

August 20, 1915

From: FWW Doane, City Engineer

To: James McGregor, Superintending Engineer

I have to protest most strenuously against your action of placing pebbles on Bower Road, Clarence St. and the roadway between Bower Road and Tower Road. The material is most unsuitable for road repairs and it is very difficult and almost impossible to get through with a motor car. It is equally unsatisfactory for team traffic, as the pebbles roll about under the horses' feet. Round stone is a most unsuitable material for road construction and repair, and I must ask you to have it removed without delay.

As I have been told by you on other occasions when I have spoken to you about some things in connection with the work that the contractor was the responsible man, I beg to call your attention to one or two clauses in your specification which in my opinion place the responsibility upon yourself—Section 5 provides that the work shall be carried on in such a manner as the Engineer shall direct and to his satisfaction. Section 11 provides that the work shall in every particular be under and subject to the control and supervision of the Engineer and the contractor shall obey promptly any orders, directions or instructions at any time given by the Engineer. Section 22 provides that the contractor shall use due care that no person or property is injured.

Now, as you are practically the Czar of the whole work (I use the term with no offensive meaning) I beg to call your attention to the fact that the workmen are proceeding with the coyoting work at Young Avenue, although I am informed that an injunction has been issued by the court against it. When the contractor did this kind of blasting a short distance west of Young Avenue, a large quantity of rock was thrown out on the other side of the cutting, that is the north side, where it can be seen today, and the destructive effect on the trees in its path is also a witness to the danger of such work. I and my family have had to live under very trying conditions for many months, but this latest menace is the "last straw." I am informed by one of the lawyers who was handling the injunction case that you claim to have nothing to do with it but that it is the contractor only. I shall be glad to hear your method of evading a responsibility which the specification places upon you.

I write not only in my own personal interest, but officially in the interest of my neighbors and the public.

Both these matters are serious and urgent and I beg that you will give them your immediate attention.

August 23, 1915

From: George B. Low, Local Building Contractor

To: FWW Doane, City Engineer

I have a contract for concrete work at a residence on Young Avenue, south of the railway ditch. There is no access to Young Avenue except by a bridge across the ditch at the Bowery Road. Some party has dumped a large quantity of beach pebbles, like marbles, at both ends of bridge on the roadway. It is impossible to haul a full load over this road. Will you kindly give the matter your attention, as I wish to commence hauling over the road at once.

August 23, 1915

From: Fred Monaghan, City Clerk

To: Board of Control Minutes

Mr. Pearson and Ralph P. Bell appeared before and addressed the Board on this matter and also bad conditions on Bower Road due to a quantity of material placed on the road by the contractors of the Ocean Terminals. Pearson stated that the placing of this material on the road was a violation of the Dominion Railway Act.

The City Engineer informed the Board that he had written to the Superintending Engineer of the Ocean Terminals to remove said material from the roadway.

August 23, 1915

From: James McGregor, Superintending Engineer

To: FWW Doane, City Engineer

I am in receipt of your letter of the 20th inst., from which I note your objections to the gravel which we have placed on our temporary roads east of "Maple-wood."

Will you please advise me by what authority you are asking me to have gravel removed from temporary roads on Government lands which have not been handed over to the City and for the maintenance of which, as I understand it, the Government Railways are at present responsible?

If, as requested in my letter to you of the 20th inst. the City will cooperate with us in having these roads rolled with their steam road roller there is no reason why very excellent road surfaces should not be obtained.

In the frequently recurring subject of inconvenience, annoyance and damage to your house and yourself and your family, I have advised you that the contractors are, under their contract with the Government, responsible for any damage done by their operations.

I am not aware of ever having tried to evade any responsibility that properly rests upon me as Engineer and as regards what you have learned by hearsay it would of course be ridiculous for me to accept any responsibility.

As regards coyote holes, I am not aware of any injunction which prevents us from driving any coyote or other holes on our Government lands.

August 24, 1915

From: FWW Doane, City Engineer

To: George B. Low

I beg to acknowledge receipt of your letter of 23rd inst. I have sent a copy of it to Mr. James McGregor, the engineer in charge of the Terminal work. I have already protested to Mr. McGregor against the use of such material but he claims that a very excellent road can be made with it, and practically tells me that it is none of my business as the most of it is government property. Under the circumstances I regret that I cannot at present do anything to help you out.

August 24, 1915

From: FWW Doane, City Engineer

To: James McGregor, Superintending Engineer

I beg to acknowledge receipt of your letter of 23rd inst. I am rather surprised that you should take the stand apparently that I have no right to ask you to move the round, pebbly beach gravel which you have placed on the roads in the vicinity of the railway cutting. However, I have not the slightest objection to telling you what I consider my authority.

In the first place, I have been instructed by the Board of Control to take this matter up on complaint of a number of citizens. I am sending you enclosed, a copy of one letter with my reply. These roads, whether on Government property or not, are being maintained by you for the benefit of the public and not only for the benefit of the Government, and in addition, Clarence Street is one of the streets on which these pebbles were used and I am not aware that the Government has taken that street. Chapter 76 Revised Statutes of Canada respecting Government Railways section 15 sub-section 2 states:

"No obstruction of such highway with the works shall be made without diverting the highway so as to leave an open and good passage for carriages and on the completion of the works the highway shall be replaced."

You have opened a passage, but to say that, in its present condition, it is a good one for carriages, which includes all vehicles, is more than any fair-minded man could say truthfully. That also, is my authority for acting in the interest of the public.

While we are on the matter I have to call your attention to your neglect to provide a diversion in place of the highway at Young Avenue. It is true that you have provided a foot-bridge and I anticipate that that will be your reply; also that you may say that the bridge on Bower Road meets this requirement of the Act, but sub-section 4 states:

"This section shall not limit or interfere with the powers of the Minister to divert or alter any road, street or way when another road is substituted in lieu thereof."

I am informed by the City Solicitor that the fact that so many people are complaining is prima facie evidence that the other bridge is not a convenient way. This also should be apparent to any fair-minded man, as the extra distance which it is necessary to travel in order to use it to get to that part of the city formerly reached by Young Avenue, is to say the least, not convenient. This extra distance is a serious handicap in case of fire.

Respecting your request for the use of the City steam road roller, I cannot endorse the making of roads as you propose, in the first place; and in the second place, I could not advise risking the steam roller over your bridge, the safety of which I am informed, has already been questioned.

Regarding the coyote holes, I do not for one moment question your right to drive such holes, but the fact that you are driving them indicates to me that there has been intention to disregard the Order of the Court; hence, my protest. Further, I must take your letter as an endorsement of the work as you do not disdain any such intention but your manner of replying to my protest indicates that you are in sympathy with the course the contractor is following. This, of course, should go without saying, as you are in sole control of the work under the contract, and the contractor must obey any instructions given by you.

As this correspondence is most unsatisfactory to me and I have been asked by the Board of Control to report on the matter, I am sending a copy of the correspondence to them. I regret exceedingly that your letters show no disposition to discuss such matters with a view to arriving at a solution which will be satisfactory to the public as well as to Government interests. I have no desire to hamper your work in any way, but in my work, I am obliged to listen to the opinion of every man who feels inclined to criticize, and in doing so I have discovered over and over again that criticism could be well founded and that engineering opinion is not necessarily infallible.

August 24, 1915

From: FWW Doane, City Engineer

To: Mayor Peter Martin

I beg to report respecting complaints that have been made against the use of round, pebbly beach gravel for repairing the roads and road diversions in the vicinity of the railway cuttings in Young Avenue and Bower Road.

I have had some correspondence with Mr. McGregor respecting the matter, copy of which is attached. I am also attaching copy of letter from Mr. C. B. Low with copy of my reply.

Although Mr. McGregor informed Mr. Pearson, one of those complaining, in a letter about the 12th of August, that in all their arrangements they were endeavouring to carry out their work to the satisfaction of the Board of Control and City Council, as the responsible representatives of the public, I regret to say that I have been able to make no progress that would satisfy the public; in fact Mr. McGregor in his latest letter questions my authority to ask him to remove the objectionable material and since I made the request, he has made the roads much worse than they were before.

It would be very difficult, and in my judgement impossible, to get the heavy fire engines through this material with their regular team, and if the engines were to stall there and extra teams had to be obtained, the situation would not be an attractive one, as damage undoubtedly would be caused in case of fire, that might be prevented if the roadway were in better condition for such traffic.

The roads are a serious handicap to a builder like Mr. Low, as no team can haul a heavy load through the pebbles. I think the Board will have to take some step which will ensure recognition of the public interest, as my efforts have failed entirely.

Respecting bridges, I have not been able to enquire thoroughly into the safety of the bridge at Bower Road. As your Board are aware, Mr. Pearson's information that it is the intention not to make the bridge on Young Avenue the full width of the roadway and sidewalks is correct, and protest has already been made to the Minister of Railways. I heard of this intention accidently, as the Supervising Engineer is making his bridge plans without consulting me. It has been his policy to make his plan first, then ask for approval and if we refuse it, to protest against our attitude, regardless of our opinion as to the requirements in the City's interests.

As the Terminal Engineer hints that we have no authority to question his right to do the work as he sees fit, regardless of the opinion of the public, I would suggest that the City Solicitor be asked to give his opinion on this point.

Mr. Pearson stated that the placing of the material on the road was a violation of the Dominion Railway Act.

August 26, 1915

From: Controller

To: James McGregor

Re Condition Bower Road and Clarence Street

Referring to correspondence passing between our Engineer and yourself in regard to the material used on the above, we feel that it is unnecessary for us to further point out the danger and inconvenience that same is causing the City, and feel satisfied that you will appreciate our position in the matter, and have immediate steps taken to correct same.

The report made by the Chief of the Fire Department in regard to the impossibility of apparatus getting over these roads is one which makes necessary we ask that the matter be given the earliest possible attention, and we would appreciate your having us advised just when same will be taken up and suitable material supplied to put these roads in passable condition.

A line in this connection at your earliest convenience will oblige.

‡‡‡‡‡‡‡‡‡‡‡‡‡‡‡‡

More than two years after he started sparring with the contractors and James McGregor, FWW headed off to war. At the beginning of June 1916, City Council granted him a leave of absence for the period of the war and for six months thereafter should his services be required for that length of time.

One of his final missives on the subject of the three bridges was on March 22, 1916, with a note to the mayor:

> The Terminal railway authorities began this morning to remove the foot bridge across the railway cut near Young Avenue.
>
> As there have been statements made relating to myself, which are not in accordance with the facts, in connection with this work, I desire to place on record beyond question, my position regarding the matter.
>
> I have not approved of and do not approve of the change proposed by Mr. McGregor. The work could be carried on by taking out the rock up to Young Avenue and then erecting a trestle bridge across the cut below the street, so that the existing bridge could be removed. I have the assurance that this can be done, by one of the most prominent officials of the contractors. As the change being made will be most unsatisfactory to the residents below the railway and others using the street, I do not wish to have the impression go abroad that I have approved of it.

CHAPTER 13

CYNTHIA, ELEANOR, KING EDWARD, AND LORD KITCHENER

The shooting of the rock in the Fairview end of the cutting presented many difficulties, the rock being very faulty, containing pockets of rotten-disintegrated rock, mud, clay, gravel and sand, as well as water. The cut was drilled and shot no less than three times before it could be completely excavated.[69]

– Arthur C. Brown, Engineer

PLEASANT STREET, THE LONG STREET THAT LED ALONG THE SHORE FROM DOWNTOWN HALIFAX TO POINT Pleasant, was being denuded of buildings while the dumping of stone and gravel from more than six months of work on the railway cut went forward, pushing the shoreline out. On April 29, 1914, Halifax City Council approved the diversion of Pleasant Street to make room for the construction of a concrete-block moulding and storage yard, indicating that they would soon be making the large concrete shells that would be used as the structural members in the quay walls.

Occupants in some of the houses on Gas Lane and in the vicinity had been notified to be out by May 1, and it was expected that the Yacht Squadron property would have to be vacated early in the summer. In the area between the Esplanade and the Yacht Squadron clubhouse, the harbour water and the street had originally been separated by just a couple of metres, but by the second week of April the infilling had grown that distance to sixty metres. The filling process was happening for about a fifth of a kilometre along the shore at the northern end. Railway tracks were laid at the shoreline and used for a few days as Cook and Wheaton's trains carried rock and gravel from the rock face and dumped it into the sea. Then the tracks were taken up and re-laid and the trains repeated the process, ever expanding the shoreline to accommodate the railway yards and docks soon to be built. One hundred thousand cubic metres, with many times that still to go, had been transferred by the steam locomotives hauling cars from the rock face at Tower Road to the water's edge.

Two locomotives and a large number of automatic dumping cars were at work on this part of the job. A steam shovel did the digging and the loading of cars at the leading edge of the cut. The heavy blasting that was required at the outset near Young Avenue had been reduced on the way to Tower Road. But it would soon pick up again because the area of Tower Road was the highest point on the route, and a lot of rock would have to be dislodged. A temporary bridge was about to be built to carry Young Avenue foot traffic over the cut to Point Pleasant and the few houses that didn't need to come down, including Michael Dwyer's and FWW's.

At the other end of the cut, which commenced at the southwest corner of the Bedford Basin in Fairview Cove, progress was also respectable. The crew was working between Mumford and Bayers Roads. They were similarly equipped with dumping cars and a steam shovel to load them, and locomotives to shuttle them back and forth from the dig site to where the basin was being filled in to create a rail yard and sheds.

They called the passenger docks at the Ocean Terminals the "quay wall." When completed, it was really a submerged fortress designed to protect the land, not from invading soldiers, but from the invading North Atlantic, which could be more destructive. A century later, for a scuba diver (like yours truly) on the bottom, where people had worked inside a caisson—a large watertight chamber—using 1915 technology, it looms up and disappears into the gloom—a perfect vertical wall breaking the surface a minimum of fourteen metres above, depending on the tides. It is 9.5 metres thick and built with reinforced concrete and granite. The concrete consists of shells that were so big they had

These large concrete shells were used as the structural members in the quay walls; in this image, they have been newly removed from the moulds and are waiting for the concrete to be fully cured before being moved to storage. After being laid into place at the outside of the infill, the honeycombed concrete blocks were locked together and filled with rock and concrete, then the outer wall covered with granite blocks. [Tom Lynskey collection]

Moving the temporary track while building the cut, six months into the project. Houses in the background, obscured by coal smoke and steam from the many engines, belong to Elizabeth Bauld, Hugh Silver, and Samuel Brookfield. [Tom Lynskey collection]

to be manufactured on-site. Because of the makeup of the bottom, the engineers decided they needed to make them as big as they could manage within the limitations of their ability to move and set them into place.

A lot of activity was going on at multiple locations. In addition to the two work gangs engaged at both ends of the railway cut, concrete blocks were being manufactured in a moulding plant erected at the Georges Island site; the concrete posts that held the blocks together were in production at a plant in Eastern Passage, across the harbour; sand was being sourced from a beach in Lawrencetown, about thirty kilometres east of Halifax; two quarries in Purcells Cove, within the harbour and about two kilometres from the site, were providing granite; and reinforcing steel was being forged at steel plants in Sydney and New Glasgow, NS.

Newly quarried granite stone blocks in Purcells Cove, bound for the finishing plant to be cut and polished in preparation for installation on the outer surface of a quay wall. [Tom Lynskey collection]

The huge reinforced-concrete blocks that would form the quay walls came with uniform openings to lock them precisely above one another when placed in the wall. The blocks were impressive—9.5 metres long, 6.7 metres wide, and 1.2 metres high—and were set in the water, one on top of another like LEGO to form a wall 9.5 metres thick and as long as needed. Long concrete locking posts ran top-to-bottom in each stack, and when all blocks were firmly locked in place the openings were filled with concrete and rubble rock, the whole thus being welded into a solid structure. An exterior wall of granite was then bonded to the outside, forming a virtually indestructible set of quays able to withstand the actions of frost, ice, wave action, and other elements—those between high and low tides as well as occasional violent contact from ships and fenders. Today they show the wear and tear of more than a century of incessant stress but are still doing the job.

Providing the shell blocks with a level, immovable place to sit on the bottom required significant preparation, including underwater blasting. Two drill boats were constructed for the job, appropriately called *Drill Boat No. 1* and *Drill Boat No. 2*. The former had seven drilling machines three metres apart and the latter had ten, giving the ability to simultaneously drill seventeen holes to receive charges. Each vessel had a boiler and a generator to enable electric lights for working at night. After the holes had been drilled, cartridges of dynamite were slipped down pipes and into the holes. With the charges set and wires attached, the drill boat moved about sixty metres away and set off the blast using a battery.

After the bottom of the ocean had been blasted to break up the rock below, the stone had to be rearranged or recovered. As with the stone and gravel from the railway trench, the contractors used robust steam-powered equipment. Moving material from underwater was different in three respects. First, the power plant was on a barge instead of railway tracks. Second, the material to be moved or recovered was far below the water surface, fifteen metres or more, so a shovel on a boom could not be used. Instead, a shovel suspended on a cable was dropped below and operated from above. Finally, the operator of a dredge could not see below, so they had to work without a visual reference.

Maritime Dredging's dipper dredge *Cynthia* rearranged the rock from the blast site on the bottom and brought any excess to the surface to be used as infill. With a maximum working depth of seventeen metres, *Cynthia* dredged between nine- and ten thousand cubic metres of material per week. A dredge named *King Edward* and owned by the W. J. Poupotre Company of Montréal was also employed dredging and filling. Equipped with a five-cubic-metre bucket, it could work at depths to fifteen metres.

> The term "diving bell" comes from the devices used for hundreds of years to safely (more or less!) put humans underwater. The first ones were shaped like a bell. If you turn an empty drinking glass upside down and push it into water, the air stays inside. Make it bigger and construct it out of bronze or steel and you have a diving bell that enables you to dwell underwater. Bottom time is limited by the size of the thing and the number of people consuming the air.

When the dredging of an area was completed, preparing the foundations required people to work underwater—either hard-hat divers or workers in a diving bell. The contractor's "bell" was a large steel chamber 12 metres by 8 metres by 2.1 metres high, provided with separate shafts and locks for people and materials. A water ballast tank enabled it to sink to 17 metres and refloat itself. Eight or ten people usually worked inside. Compressed air kept most of the water out—they waded in shallow water as they worked—and provided a living atmosphere for the workers. Breathing compressed air places limitations on bottom time, so that had to be managed.

The locks worked on the same principle used on a space station when an astronaut takes a spacewalk. If they were to simply open the door as we would on the Earth's surface, all the air would rush out, taking everything in the station with it. To avoid such a catastrophe, there is an intermediate chamber with a door to the outside and one to the inside, like a porch. The astronaut steps through the inside door into the porch and the door is closed behind them, leaving the person "locked." The astronaut then opens the outside door to emerge into space, while the inside door keeps the air and people inside.

Lowering a bucket of ready-mix concrete from the plant on the barge to men working below water level in the diving bell. One of the two drilling barges is on the right. [Tom Lynskey collection]

The bell received surface support from a wooden barge forty-six metres long by ten metres wide, fitted with high- and low-air-compression pumps, a generator to provide electric lighting for the workers below, a 0.5 cubic metre Ransome concrete mixer, sand and gravel bins, and a steam derrick for hoisting. Under good working conditions the diving bell could prepare seven linear metres of foundations per day. To build the wall's foundations, newly mixed concrete was taken into the bell through the material shaft in a bottom-dumping steel bucket and shovelled into place. To get rid of loose rock and debris recovered from the bottom, workers placed the material into a bucket that was hauled up through the material shaft. Mud and small stones were expelled with compressed air through a nine-centimetre-diameter pipe.

They used the dredges for big jobs of moving or removing rocks and mud. The dredge *Lord Kitchener* was a Marion model 281 excavator equipped with a five-cubic-metre bucket and mounted on a barge fifty-seven metres long by fourteen metres wide. *Lord Kitchener* moved on railway tracks that ran nearly the full length of the barge; it was capable of lifting ninety tons at a radius of twenty-one metres. There was also a Marion model 261 drag-line excavator called *Eleanor*, mounted on a barge forty-two metres long by eleven metres wide and equipped with a three-cubic-metre bucket.

When Henry Barnhart, Edward Huber, and George W. King started the Marion Steam Shovel Company in 1884, they did not name it after anyone's girlfriend, wife, sister, or mother. They named it after Marion, Ohio, where they lived. The company was around for more than a century and is probably best known for building the two crawler-transporters that NASA used for moving the *Saturn V* rocket, and later the space shuttles, to their launch pads.

The two government-owned quarries were at the mouth of the Northwest Arm near a village called Purcells Cove and were themselves large operations equipped with stonecutting sheds, surfacing machines, and rock-crushing plants to prepare the product. The quarries produced two grades of high-quality granite. The first was what we may call rubble—essentially barge-loads of granite rocks to employ as fill and to crush for multiple uses such as sand. The second was as the blocks for the finished faces of the quay walls; these were placed outside the concrete pieces from which the piers were constructed to protect the softer concrete from wave action and ice on the outer facing of the wall. To move the stone for preparation and then to the barges for transport to the job site, there were derricks, railway tracks, locomotives, and flatcars. The finishing and polishing of the granite stones was done in two sheds by some eighty stonecutters. After the granite blocks arrived on-site, they required additional grooming at a stonecutting plant near where Pier A had been infilled. There were four surfacing machines for cutting and dressing the granite for the facework of the quay walls.

While the foundations were being put into place, the block-moulding plant was working overtime to create sufficient blocks to supply the project throughout the winter. Because the cold prevented the blocks from being made in winter, there had to be a spacious storage yard with inventory sufficient to get them to spring, when manufacturing could begin anew.

Crews finishing the granite block facing that covers the concrete blocks at Berths 23 and 24, with Georges Island in the background. The train is dumping stone into the empty spaces in the blocks. [SOURCE UNKNOWN]

The concrete blocks needed at least a month to set before being moved. The contractors erected sufficient wooden platforms to have, at any given time, up to three hundred blocks in the process of hardening to the point where they could be handled by the crane. When completed, each block weighed about sixty-two tons, being composed of twenty-nine cubic metres of concrete and three tons of reinforcing steel. Making 2,300 of these blocks called for a total of six hundred thousand bags of cement, over ninety thousand tons of reinforcing steel (along with a shop and equipment to twist and bend the steel), nearly fifty thousand cubic metres of sand that had been purchased from a beach in Lawrencetown (some thirty kilometres away), and a hundred thousand cubic metres of stone—not to mention the copious amounts of that precious water that had to be bought and delivered.

What had been the Royal Nova Scotia Yacht Squadron clubhouse was smack in the middle of the block-moulding yard's southern perimeter, which made it an excellent location to store five thousand barrels of cement, but that only satisfied part of the requirement. A second building with another twenty thousand barrels brought in from

Ready-mix concrete pours from three mixers into containers aboard a railway car. Sand, cement, lime, and water were stored above the mixers and flowed down as needed. The containers were then moved to the block-manufacturing yard where the ready-mix was poured into moulds to make the blocks. [TOM LYNSKEY COLLECTION]

A train-mounted crane moving granite blocks from a flatcar into position on the outer layer of the quay wall. [NS ARCHIVES PHOTOGRAPHIC COLLECTION]

Montréal and Belleville was built to the south of that one to meet the cement needs of the project. The scale was so large that there were conveyors to move the sand, separators to screen out the big bits, and crushers to reduce those bits down to sand. The sand and cement eventually flowed into the three mixers, where water poured in. It all got mixed, poured into containers on railway cars, moved to the platforms, and dumped into the steel forms, where each new block sat peacefully until the train arrived a month later to take it to the storage area, where it sat until needed.

Those rail cars were manufactured in Halifax by Nova Scotia Car Works. The plant was in the middle of the city in an area bounded by North, Windsor, Almon, and Clifton Streets. Today there is a Sobeys supermarket and parking lot on the property, but before Sobeys moved in, Farmers Dairy occupied the site for many years.

The first block was set into place on the north quay of Basin No. 1 on September 25, 1915, and in the following year about 750 metres of completed wall were built. Throughout the project, an average of 82 metres of wall were constructed per month. A 150-ton crane mounted on railway tracks moved the blocks onto flatcars, which took them to the water's edge. There, the crane, after lumbering its way down to the shore, lowered them into place. This was a very dicey operation. Laying 62-ton concrete shells perfectly into place on the bottom of the ocean at least fifteen metres down and then piling them atop one another until the whole thing was four to six metres above the surface with a precision that locked them together into a smooth, durable, and perfectly vertical wall was no small feat. Once everything was stable, the hollow parts in the blocks got filled with concrete and stone from the dredging. When completed, the whole wall was a single unit reaching down over twenty metres.

Meanwhile, in Eastern Passage on the other side of the harbour, the Nova Scotia Construction Company was busy manufacturing concrete posts for the shed foundations and the guide-and-key posts that aligned the concrete blocks underwater.

These posts are still holding those blocks in position today.

CHAPTER 14

BUILDING BRIDGES

No plans have been submitted to me, and I have no information to show me how the railway engineers propose to deal with the crossings of streets.[70]

– FWW Doane, City Engineer

THE FIRST TIME I TURNED ONTO THE NORTH HALF OF CONNAUGHT AVENUE AS A NEW RESIDENT OF HALIFAX, I immediately perceived that I was on a significant thoroughfare. At thirty-seven metres, it is one of the widest roads in the city. I breezed along comfortably, admiring the median with its tall trees, when I suddenly had to hit the brakes. The road had ended. I found myself in a state of denial, unable to process that this beautiful and efficient piece of four-to six-lane roadway ended so abruptly for no apparent reason. There was a stop sign, and I was obliged to turn left or right onto a clogged two-lane street, while across that street was what appeared to be open space. What I didn't realize was that the railway cut was not far ahead.

It is one example of the negative effect the Ocean Terminals development had on the city. In addition to turning a large part of the peninsula into railway yards and docks and creating a trench from end to end that complicated getting around, it also changed plans for the development of a new area of Halifax. Connaught Avenue is the only boulevard through the peninsula. It was in the city plan, intended to connect with Francklyn Street, thereby enabling travel from one end of the city to the other in a line from the Bedford Basin to Point

Pleasant. Work had already begun—but it finished in the middle of nowhere. More than a hundred years later, it still has an unfinished feel, as though the city ran out of money to complete it. Connaught could have easily continued to Coburg Road, as the area there, called Conrose Park or the Horsefields, is a wide open and underused piece of parkland. Beyond that is the railway cut, followed by a conglomeration of short streets and lanes that seem to have fallen together as estates were subdivided by people who probably had lots of sway at City Hall, and one after another, they got their way. Navigating through the area is a pain to this day.

A 1930 city map shows Connaught extending to Robie Street—wishful thinking on the part of city planners, no doubt—but they were still depicting a dream, not a reality. The grand boulevard remained the stump that it is today.

My first drive through the city got worse. After the unexpected stop at the end of Connaught, I turned left on Jubilee and within a minute or two was at an intersection with Oxford Street. Then, after a right turn, more traffic lights, and multiple left and right turns (like following a staircase turned on its side), I meandered my way to Tower Road. This one finally took me over the railway cut to the entrance to Point Pleasant Park. There may be some prestige in living in Halifax's South End, but there is also a lot of inconvenience in getting there.

There are just two bridges that access the extreme South End of Halifax—Tower Road and Young Avenue—while there could easily have been four. On February 10, 1916, City Council passed a resolution to take FWW's recommendation to remind the railway that a bridge was needed to extend Robie Street to Point Pleasant Park: "This crossing was decided on by the City Council some time ago, when the street extension of Connaught Avenue from the Park to the Basin was considered. Robie Street and Connaught Avenue would join at this point."[71]

A month before construction of the bridges commenced, while plans were being finalized, FWW, in a May 25, 1916, communique to the mayor regarding the Robie Street/Connaught Avenue bridge, noted:

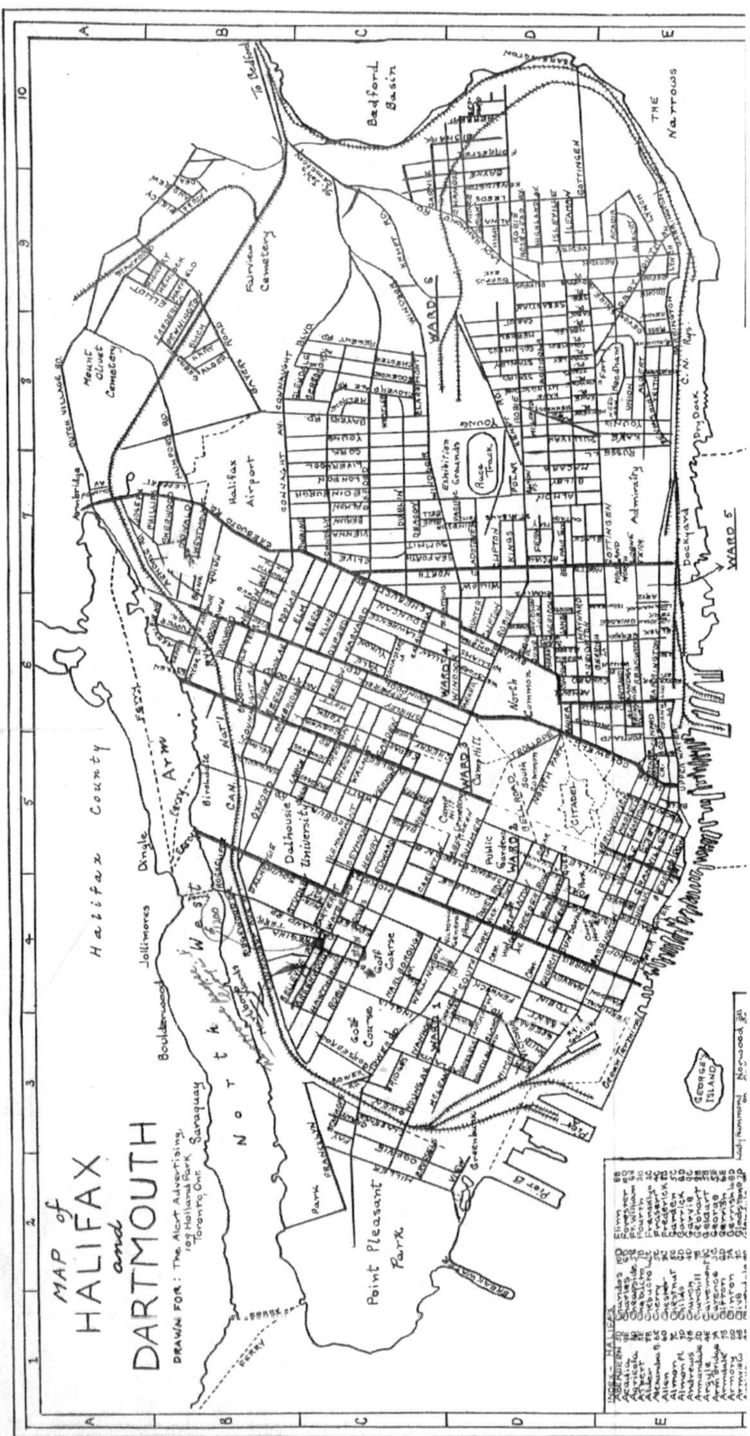

This 1930 map of Halifax shows Connaught Avenue extending all the way through the South End to Robie Street, even though Connaught actually ends at Jubilee Road. This map also depicts the rail cut interrupting Connaught's potential connection to Francklyn Street. [NS ARCHIVES MAP COLLECTION: V6 239]

> The plan for this bridge has not been signed by the General Manager [of the railway, F. P. Gutelius] and Mr. McGregor in his letter of May 1st states that it was not agreed upon. This is not in accordance with my recollection and that of [assistant city engineer] Mr. Johnston in reference to the matter. The plan of the bridge was approved–the only question was whether it should be built at once or when the street was opened. I think it is most important that the plan should be approved and that there should be some written understanding on the part of the railway authorities to construct it, so that we shall have record on which we may depend, instead of having to depend on memory.[72]

Wise words, but the bridge was never built. FWW would go off to fight overseas shortly afterward. It is probably safe to say that had he been around, the bridge would have been built and the movement of traffic in the South End of the city would be smoother today. There is not a single straight route across the 6.5-kilometre drive spanning the city from the basin to Point Pleasant. Robie Street ends literally in woods that keep you from driving into the trench. It isn't the only street that ends abruptly. In parallel, Oxford Street/Beaufort Avenue also ends in the same woods for the same reason.

The Young Avenue bridge was one of the biggest sources of contention of the whole project. It was the longest because of the multiple pairs of tracks below as the gap widens into the yard. That made it the most intricate and expensive. It was part of a boulevard that was to become the most exclusive street in the city, leading from Inglis Street to Point Pleasant Park. Young Avenue's glory blossomed in the twentieth century and has now faded, owing to developers who demolished some big historic houses, including the home of George Campbell, while nobody at City Hall was noticing. It's the story of all Canadian cities—Halifax is no exception.

Michael Dwyer, FWW Doane, and three-time alderman Alfred Whitman were in an exposed location. In March 1917 they had been waiting three years for the bridge over the tracks to be built to put Young Avenue back together. The railway, the city, the Civic Improvement League, and the bridge designers—Ross & Macdonald of Montréal — were bogged down over how wide the sidewalks should be.[73]

In a long report to the mayor on March 16, 1917, acting city engineer H. W. Johnston concluded:

> Some of the residents on Young Avenue and the public using the Park, have probably been put to more inconvenience than those on any other street in the City, owing to the obstruction to traffic due to the construction of the railway, and the Department of Railways should be asked to proceed with the construction of this bridge immediately.[74]

The issue was the bridge's width. The street was wide for the time, and the railway, looking to save money, decided the bridge could be narrower than the road. That was hard to slip by FWW. Early on, he made a convincing case that yes, the street was wide, but the city was growing, and this was an important artery and the main entrance to the park. He contended that the Young Avenue bridge should be eighty feet (twenty-four metres) wide to allow for extra-wide sidewalks. Even the Civic Improvement League, under George Campbell who, like FWW, had invested in a large house on the street, thought that was a bit over the top. Campbell argued for sixty feet (eighteen metres).

So along with fighting with the railway, the two most powerful men in the ring—usually in agreement—were squabbling with one another. FWW's opinion prevailed, and now, for more than a century, pedestrians heading to the park have had a comfortably wide space as they cross the attractive bridge and approach the homes once occupied by City Engineer Doane, Board of Trade President Michael Dwyer, and retired lawyer Alfred N. Whitman, all of whom suffered anything but meekly for more than three years and whose quiet and palatial neighbourhood was forever altered.

The project plan called for sixteen bridges; virtually all articles written since that time declare that sixteen were built, but I have not been able to account for sixteen bridges. Today, there are bridges over or under the following streets: the Bedford Highway, Bayers Road, Bicentennial Highway, Mumford Road, Chebucto Road, Quinpool Road, Prince Arthur Street, Jubilee Road, Coburg Road, South Street, Oakland Road, Belmont Road, Marlborough Road, Tower Road, and

Above left: The former home of City Engineer FWW Doane. Above right: The home of former Halifax Board of Trade president, Michael Dwyer. Below: The former home of Alfred N. Whitman. All three houses still stand today on Young Avenue in Halifax, having endured the many challenges posed by the construction of the rail cut. [AUTHOR PHOTOS]

The Quinpool Road bridge, nearing completion in November 1916. Three workers are delivering gravel by train, which they shovel into a bucket to be raised to the bridge's surface. [HALIFAX MUNICIPAL ARCHIVES, MACLACHLAN PHOTO CR6-122.41]

Young Avenue. That makes fifteen, but the Bicentennial Highway was built many years later, so only fourteen were built then, twelve of them in 1917 by Cook and Wheaton. Bridges at Chebucto Road and the Bedford Highway carried the tracks over the road and were built by the Maritime Bridge Company.

In addition to causing bad blood between the city and the railway, the areas around the bridges were an opportunity for injury and a temptation for vandalism. Lawyer John J. Power reported to the mayor on July 21, 1916:

> The temporary driveway connecting Coburg Road with the temporary driveway bridge over the cutting near the Waegwoltic is unprotected by the electric lights strung there, which were not lit last night, and persons travelling in automobiles run the risk of driving through the frail fence netting into the sixty-foot

> cut. The place should be lighted, as lights are provided there, but the place was in darkness last night. This neglect is a menace to human life.[75]

City Clerk Fred Monaghan contacted the contractor, and Andrew Wheaton complained about vandalism on the sites, including broken lamps, cut wires, and the electric switches being messed with. "We use our very best endeavors to keep the lights on at all times, but it is almost impossible to guard against people who interfere with our system," Wheaton told the Board of Control.[76] In that case, the electrician reported that the lights over a two-kilometre stretch had been put out of commission.

Wheaton had no cause to complain, however, because two years previously the chief of police had called to James McGregor's attention that there was insufficient security at the site, noting that there had been several reports of women being "molested" near the South End section. He recommended that four "special policemen" be engaged. McGregor responded by suggesting that Cook and Wheaton employ their watchmen in the role. The police chief insisted that he should contract with the city to use the Halifax Police. A year later, Cook and Wheaton finally engaged one special constable.

CHAPTER 15

JOINING LAND AND SEA IN HALIFAX

Halifax is not only "the warden of the honor of the North," but it is the one port through which European mails for the whole North American continent can be received and transmitted with the greatest possible dispatch.[77]

– Halifax Board of Trade

IN THE GLORY DAYS OF PASSENGER STEAMSHIPS, THERE WERE TWO CARGOES THAT THE SHIPPING LINES relied on: mail and immigrants. The oldest and most basic communication medium of human civilization over long distances is the mail, and the consistent, reliable, and secure handling of the mail has been one of the most important concerns of nations. The mail is key to doing business, and being associated with its care is also good for business. When Halifax entrepreneur Samuel Cunard set out to create the world's biggest and longest-lasting shipping line, he knew that securing the contract for carrying the mail across the Atlantic Ocean for the world's largest empire would be his key to success. Having a ship that carried the mail conveyed so much prestige that it was part of the ship's name. Everybody has heard of, not just the *Titanic*, but the RMS *Titanic*. It was a Royal Mail Ship. Being the port that the mail moved through also carried a certain cachet. Halifax had enjoyed that privilege for thirty-six years.

With sugar refining, textile manufacturing, and increased shipbuilding, the city's manufacturing base was growing, and the solution to the harbour woes was settled at last. The power brokers of Halifax were feeling buoyant. In addition to the whopping new project under way, the ICR's spending on Halifax infrastructure had risen and three new shipping lines were calling at Halifax. That year, the vote of confidence from the Government of Canada had made the case for Halifax as the mail port rock-solid, but although they had confidence in their business case, the Board of Trade knew that governments can be fickle.

In the winter of 1914, with construction racing along, one menace still endured—the problem of political interference. Experience had shown that Halifax was the preferred port to handle the mail, even when its rail infrastructure had been less than ideal. With updated railways and new docks coming, those who transported the mail to and from Canada had let it be known that they wanted to continue using Halifax as the winter mail port. For the present, there was no stopping the river ports when the St. Lawrence was open. Geography was on their side, but come winter, Halifax was the logical port for sending and receiving the mail between the seat of Empire and Canada.

There was a third contender, however, and in the winter of 1914 the shipping companies were forced to use that port half the time: Saint John, NB. Saint John was closer to Montréal and was served by rail, but its location in the Bay of Fundy presented unique challenges. The nine-metre tides had to be contended with, which meant that arriving and leaving the port had to be carefully scheduled. Getting there meant navigating around western Nova Scotia, where many ships had been snagged by the strong currents and shallow water, including the SS *Hungarian*, which was carrying the Canadian mail to Portland, Maine, on February 19, 1860, when it struck the treacherous ledges off Cape Sable.

So that was another risk. And finally, the big one: Even though it was closer to Montréal by land, it was farther away from Europe by sea. The Canadian government was spending a million dollars a year to subsidize the movement of mail to and from the United Kingdom via Liverpool and Bristol. Using Saint John added 225 miles to the Liverpool route and 280 to the Bristol route. The result was that it took longer for ships from Europe to get to Saint John than to Halifax. Like most of Atlantic Canada, it also got its share of fog.

Well, why wasn't Saint John eliminated as a contender? Politics. New Brunswicker Sir Douglas Hazen was the federal minister of Marine and Fisheries and he was powerful enough to ensure that half the mail business went to Saint John. George Campbell summed it up in more colourful terms for the Board of Trade:

> And Saint John holds the business, in spite of the fact every steamer which goes there protests against it and every mail is delayed from 9 to 30 hours because the mail steamers are compelled to go there in order to butter Mr. Hazen's political parsnips.[78]

All four mail-carrying lines—Canadian Pacific, the Allan Line, the Royal Line, and the White Star Line—specified that they preferred to travel to and from Halifax. That didn't stop Saint John's politicos. They put the screws to Hazen. At a public meeting it was suggested that if he didn't do something to get the business for his city, he should resign. Nodding heads and loud applause ensued—and Hazen delivered. Royal, Allan, and White Star ships were henceforth obliged to pick up and deliver at least some of the mail at Saint John.

The Halifax business community was ticked, not only because they wanted their port to have the business, but also because the mail was delayed. *The Morning Chronicle* fumed,

> He has compelled the people of Canada, including the good people of St. John, to wait from 9 to 30 hours longer for their British mails, and he has been a party to preventing the people of Canada from getting full value for the million dollars which they pay to have their mails delivered with despatch.[79]

Mail bound for Nova Scotia and Prince Edward Island had to be sent back over territory it had already crossed, causing it to require one to two days longer to arrive at its destination.

The problem was bigger than simply disgruntled Haligonians. The poor service was being felt elsewhere in Canada. On January 22, 1914, Rodolphe Lemieux rose in the House of Commons to present the grievances of businesspeople in Toronto and Montréal. He had once been the postmaster general and was a natural person to whom the aggrieved could turn with their frustrations. He read excerpts from letters that presented similar sentiments to those in the Maritimes and urged the government to take action.

To do an end run around the problem, he hinted at turning the clock back, asking if mail marked "via New York" could be routed through New York, or was all mail now being routed through Canadian ports? Honourable Louis-Philippe Pelletier, the postmaster general, reluctantly assured him that the New York option was still open but hastened to blame the delay on two new Allan Line ships entering the service, which had caused strikes and business disruption elsewhere and was affecting the Canadian mail. Those ships were the *Alsatian* and the *Calgarian*, the largest ships in the Canadian Atlantic trade. He hinted that when the current contract ended in May, the federal government might dump the Allan Line, which had been carrying the mail since 1856. He was unaware that Canadian Pacific had quietly purchased the Allan Line in 1909 and would have been shocked to learn that competition for carrying the Canadian mail was not as healthy as he had been assuming.

To sustain their case, the Halifax Board of Trade released a pamphlet called *Halifax: Canada's Atlantic Winter Mail Port*. To demonstrate the advantages of using Halifax, it showed that time was saved over Saint John and New York no matter which of the accepted routes was used to cross the Atlantic.

The current contract was set to expire at the end of April. George Campbell was pushing the Board of Trade and local politicians to send a delegation to Ottawa and to lobby hard to avoid repeating the mistake—allowing the companies carrying the mail to select the port they wanted to use—that had been made with the last contract. All four companies had selected Halifax. It seemed simple enough, until Hazen leaned on them to change their selections. Campbell wanted to make sure that the new contract specified that the port of call would be Halifax, period, thereby not providing any other options.

It was time for the go-to fix, a delegation to Ottawa. Halifax Deputy Mayor William R. Powell led this one, departing April 27, 1914; three Board of Trade executive members went with him. When they arrived in Ottawa, they learned that the contract again enabled the steamship companies to decide which port they wanted to use. While that might have sounded innocent enough because they had chosen Halifax in the past, they had also again been yanked around by Hazen. There was still time to press their case, so they hurried back to Halifax and enlisted City Council to submit a resolution presenting their evidence to the government, drawing on research endorsed by the postmaster general himself that concluded mail sent through Halifax enjoyed a twelve-hour advantage over other Atlantic ports.

That did the trick, and all winter mail was again routed through Halifax.

Throughout the early history of Halifax, people arriving by sea typically intended to stay in Nova Scotia. Otherwise, they would have sailed up the St. Lawrence River or gone to Saint John. The coming of Confederation and the ICR had opened a new option for travellers. It meant that immigrants bound for anywhere in what had just become Canada could arrive at Halifax, get on the train, and head for the Canadian heartland, which stretched from Quebec City to Sarnia, ON. Being the winter mail port—operating from late November to mid-May—made Halifax the winter immigrant port as well.

Beginning in 1881, immigrants had arrived at the brand-new Deep Water Terminus and had been processed in the immigration facility at the original Pier 2. It was a bit of an ordeal. Going from the warmth of the ship into a cargo shed that had at best—a coal stove for heat during the brutal Canadian winter was a shock. If they were carrying a lot of luggage or had small children, it was gruelling.

By 1890, things had improved with the construction of a purpose-built immigration facility that included a small building nearby with a kitchen and an eating area, along with sleeping accommodations. That setup was short-lived, however. At 10:00 A.M. on February 27, 1895, a fire flared up in the north freight shed and two hours later the wooden buildings comprising freight sheds, machine shop, and grain elevator, along with four hundred tons of valuable freight, had gone up in a spectacular fire that destroyed a significant percentage of Deep Water Terminus assets. It developed so fast and was so fierce that tugs had to rescue people trapped on the outer end of the wharf. During all that, an explosion in the grain elevator blew people off their feet—and one through a window—but miraculously, there were no deaths. The city was within an inch of burning before everyone's eyes because the Deep Water Terminus had been jammed into the city alongside streets full of wooden houses. Many homeowners were scrambling to get their furniture out the back door as their houses were getting scorched on the front, but no houses were lost thanks to the efforts of Halifax firefighters.

After that, passengers were forced to land at Cunard's wharf nearby and make their way to the North Street railway station for processing. When things got too busy, some of them had to be taken to the Richmond Terminal a couple of kilometres away. That got the immigration department through the winter, but barely. Three short months later, the Richmond Terminal had a similar experience when a fire developed overnight into the early hours of Sunday, May 19, 1895. The biggest wharf burned to the waterline, with the loss of twenty rail cars; all the infrastructure of the city's only remaining ship-coaling service was gone, and fifty-six live cattle had succumbed. Because it was so far away, it took a long time to get horse-drawn firefighting resources to the scene. *The Halifax Herald* noted, "It is cause for celebration that the north end was not swept away."[80] With the loss of the biggest dock at the terminal, berthing for four steamships was gone. With Deepwater out of commission, the ICR was down to just two berths.

By February 1897, the ICR had new immigration quarters at the Old Pier 2. The building had been quickly put up after the fire and was a poorly constructed building atop a rebuilt dock that, in addition to settling and throwing the building out of kilter, was short and angled, making it a tight squeeze for larger passenger liners. Steamship companies preferred to land their passengers at Pier 3, next door. It was longer and had more space for the ship to manoeuvre, but it was not good for landing passengers; they were forced to walk across railway tracks and through busy freight-handling areas to get to the immigration quarters, which was just an open shed where people could evade being processed altogether. On top of that, there was no detention area in which to keep immigrants who did not meet the entry criteria.

To deal with these deficiencies, a second storey was added in 1905. Passengers and baggage were then examined on the upper level and the lower level was modified to serve passengers who had cleared inspection and were waiting to join their trains. In this area were ticket agents, a dining room, and an area for the passengers to wait.

Immigration to Canada was growing rapidly and the new building functioned well. Unfortunately, the issues with the dock remained, so in 1911 the Department of Railways and Canals decided to replace Pier 2 with a much larger dock and new sheds, along with updated immigration facilities. Construction took longer than planned. That travellers who landed at Halifax could reach their destinations faster than by any other route was again demonstrated in the summer of 1913. Passengers who landed at Halifax from the steamship *Abraham Lincoln* arrived by rail in Chicago before those who went directly to New York on the same ship had even boarded their trains in New York.[81]

By the end of 1913—a year that saw over four hundred thousand immigrants enter Canada—the new concrete Pier 2 was in place, but another two years would have to pass before the new shed and immigration quarters built on that pier were ready for use. The first ship to dock at the new Pier 2 was the Furness Withy liner *Digby* on January 20, 1914. This was a period of intense activity at the port, with sixteen liners coming and going in just four days. In the month of May 1914 twenty-five thousand immigrants landed at Halifax, compared with eleven thousand in the previous May. In earlier years, the season was generally over by May, when steamers switched to the St. Lawrence route, but in 1914 the St. Lawrence ships were running with full loads, obliging people to travel in ships bound for Halifax and Saint John.

The new immigration facility opened in the fall of 1915. Because it was not a rebuild of the previous Pier 2, which was still around, the two docks were identified as Pier 2 and Old Pier 2. Pier 2 was designed to serve passengers from two ships at a time and provided safe access to trains inside the shed.

With improved passenger safety and comfort and greatly improved security, this latest site was completed not a moment too soon. With the First World War raging, there was a lot of travel in both directions between Halifax and Europe. Two-thirds of the 425,000 Canadian soldiers who went overseas during the war departed from Halifax. The facilities were severely stressed when thousands of soldiers at a time were loading onto one of the giant four-stackers like the *Mauretania* and *Olympic*. Not all of the soldiers came back but many did, either on troop ships or hospital ships. A reception hospital helped ease the transition from ship to train for injured and disabled soldiers.

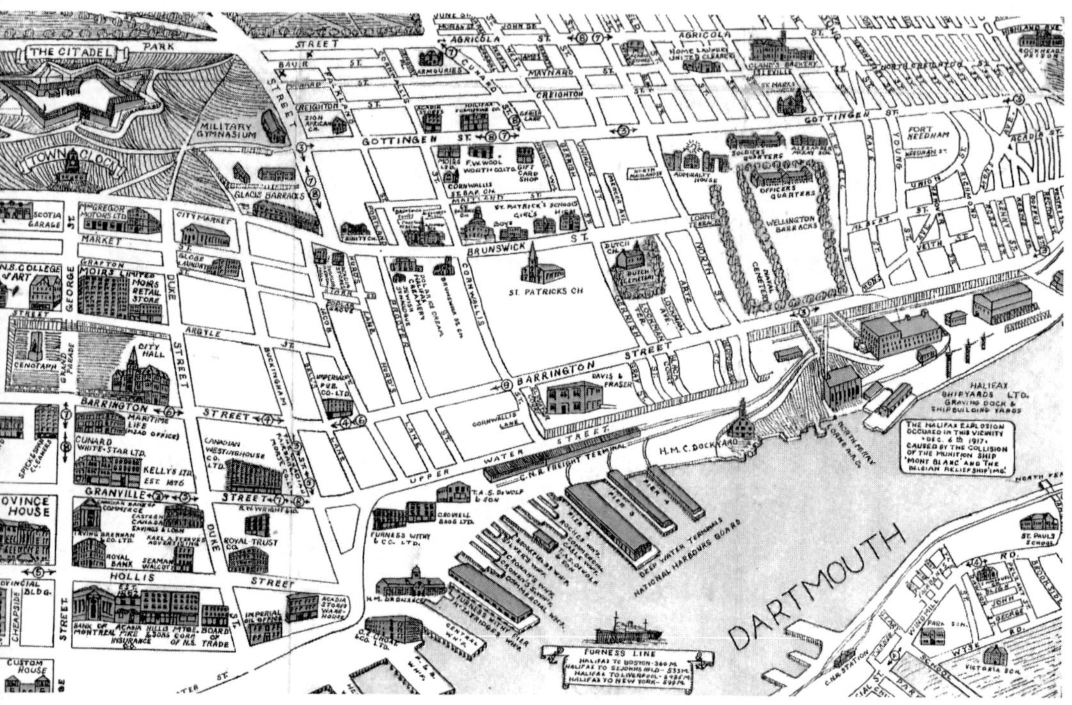

A 1930s Halifax map depicting the location of Piers 2, 3, and 4.
[HALIFAX MUNICIPAL ARCHIVES CR10-025]

CHAPTER 16

THE TEMPEST

Regret to inform you that your son William has been killed in action, nobly doing his duty for his country.[82]

– Telegram to FWW and Alice Doane, October 8, 1916

LIEUTENANT WILLIAM EDWARD EVERETT DOANE, THE YOUNGER OF FWW'S TWO CHILDREN, WAS TWENTY-three and had just earned his law degree from Dalhousie University when he was killed at the Battle of the Somme on October 1, 1916. In an unfortunate coincidence, his heartsick father had to board the troopship *Olympic*, sister ship of the *Titanic*, and depart for England on October 13 for his own war service. He had applied to City Council in May for a leave of absence until the end of the war, and for six months thereafter should his services be required. He missed the memorial service for "Billie" at a packed Fort Massey United Church on the 29th, where 250 of the 63rd Rifles gathered to honour a soldier who Robert Johnston, the regiment chaplain, called one of their youngest and most honoured officers. FWW's other son Harvey would survive his time at the front.

H. W. Johnston became the acting city engineer. Just a few weeks earlier, FWW's old nemesis, James McGregor, the superintending engineer for the project, had also been called up; he would serve as chief engineer for the 239th Battalion of the Canadian Expeditionary Force under the command of Colonel J. W. Stewart, the Stewart of Foley, Welsh, and Stewart.[83] McGregor achieved the rank of major. He finished with the project in September 1916 and was replaced by W. A. Duff, assistant chief engineer of CGR, who, a few weeks later was being credited by Andrew Wheaton with bringing new energy to the project. They were hiring ten people a day and his company would soon have five hundred workers on the job. With its usual grandiloquence, the *Herald* declared, “Before the snow falls, trains will be running to the terminals and three berths will be ready, capable of taking care of the biggest ships that float.”[84]

On the day that FWW and Alice received the sad news about their son, war came closer than ever to Halifax. On October 8, 1916, German submarine *U-53* sank five steamships off the northeast coast of the United States, just south of Nova Scotia. One of them, the *Stephano*, on its last trip of the season, was travelling from Halifax to New York and had been tied up at G. S. Campbell’s wharf just days before, having arrived from St. John’s in record time. This sinking was distressing news, not only for the loss of the ships; it was proof that submarines, a new weapon of war, could now operate off North America. Military authorities in Halifax immediately called on the mayor to implement a lights-out policy requiring the city to go into blackout conditions for the next two weeks while they assessed the risks. Further crackdowns followed, with a second submarine net being deployed at the harbour mouth between McNabs Island and the end of the new breakwater, complicating the movement of the barges carrying stone from Purcells Cove.

On November 8, 1916, at a special 11:00 A.M. meeting of Halifax City Council, Mayor Peter F. Martin presented Captain Randall of the SS *Sheba* with a gold-headed cane bearing the inscription, “Presented by the Mayor and Corporation of the City of Halifax to Captain R. Randall upon the occasion of his ship, the SS *Sheba*, being the first ocean going vessel to dock at the new Halifax Ocean Terminals Railway Piers, November 4th, 1916.” Beaming in the background were the usual suspects: F. W. Cowie, W. S. Davidson, VP of the Board of Trade, representatives of the contractors, bigwigs from the railway, and supportive aldermen.

Six weeks later, the mayor and guests were reminded that there was still work to be done in making the Ocean Terminals seaworthy. On

July 10, 1915, a couple of Foley et al.'s big barges had dragged their anchors in a summer storm and had to be rescued by tugs before they crashed into Georges Island. Much worse was in store sixteen months later as the capricious Halifax climate handed a plum to the naysayers, who had said from the start that the Ocean Terminals site was too exposed to the Atlantic. A storm blew in and did significant damage to the unfinished and very exposed docks. For those who had opposed the ambitious and expensive undertaking, it was an "I told you so" moment. But the damage had not happened because of a poor design; port authorities needed the docking space—and they had taken a shortcut.

‡‡‡‡‡‡‡‡‡‡‡‡‡‡

It was the height of the First World War, and the harbour was busier than it had ever been. Being the closest mainland North American port to Europe and one of the largest in the world, Halifax was keeping a steady stream of supplies in the form of foodstuffs, armaments, ammunition, and fresh troops flowing to the war theatre. Ships from as far away as Australia and New Zealand were constantly arriving and departing. Docking space was at a premium and the authorities decided to start using the partially completed piers.

That was not a good idea.

In the middle of 1916, the federal government decided to erect temporary sheds alongside three berths at the new terminals to load shipments during the upcoming winter. That created a disruption to the schedule of the construction, as the contractors had to focus all their resources on meeting that vital objective. With Frank Cochrane breathing down their necks, job number one was to get the seaward, or southern, end of the 610-metre seawall completed. That seawall today is home to berths now known as Piers 20, 21, and 22. At right angles to Pier 22, facing the Atlantic Ocean, are Berths 23 and 24. That was the area that had to be completed.

By December 1916 that job was done, and there was space for two ships to tie up. South of that, Pier A was built, the first of the five large wharves planned. To meet the government's emergency timetable, that dock went out only half of the 380-metre distance it would eventually go, but it still created a snug Basin No. 1 between Pier A and the berths. With the third berth on the north side of Pier A and the basin dredged to its required depth there was plenty of space to safely tie up three ships—two on the north side and one on the south.

However, they had created a problem. By not completing Pier A to its full length, they had left a large area of the north seawall, Berth 23, on the other side of the basin, exposed to the North Atlantic. A person standing on that corner of the dock could look out and see nothing but horizon between McNabs Island and the tip of the new breakwater they had built at Point Pleasant Park. The breakwater was meant to be the first of five barricades to stop the storms from invading the Ocean Terminals, but it was out there all alone and there was a lot of open water between it and the shortened Pier A. Pier A could fend off the

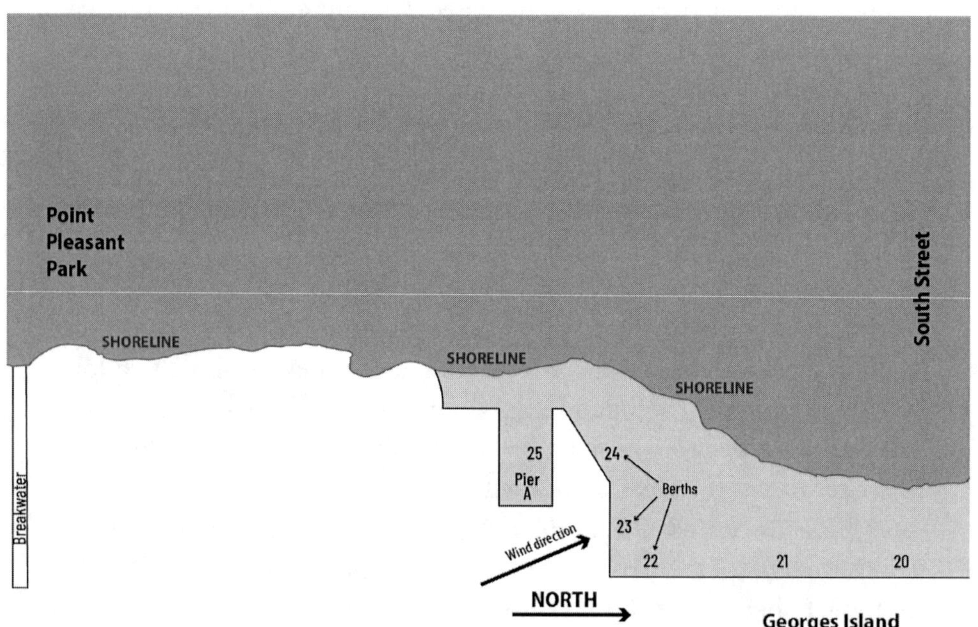

Because Pier A had not been completed to its full length, a large area of Berth 23, on the other side of the basin, was exposed to the North Atlantic. When a storm struck in December 1916, the huge waves striking Berth 23 were deflected into the dead-end space at Berths 24 and 25, creating violent chaos.
[AUTHOR SKETCH]

worst weather and keep the ships safe, but it could do nothing against the deflected water that might hit the north seawall and come barging into the basin.

Preparations were not yet complete, even for the temporary berths, when a few days before December 15 two large steamships docked at the north side of Basin No. 1. The fenders intended to be inserted between the ships and the granite wall of the dock to prevent damage to the ships were not ready, and mooring hooks and posts had not been installed. To complicate matters, the ships were tied up in an area where the vessels being used by the contractors were normally kept, so those vessels were also in need of shelter. There was nowhere else to go, so the basin between the docks quickly became a jumble of large barges closely packed beside the ships. No problem—in fine weather.

But the fenders should have been ready before any vessels had been tied up. All the two captains could obtain to insert between their ships and the granite walls of the docks were a few short hemlock timbers bound with wires. In the low visibility, they were obliged to attach their moorings to anything that offered the least hope of steadying the heavy lines.

Around midnight on December 15, 1916, high winds from the southeast—the worst possible direction because the waves could get pushed along a narrow channel that the breakwater didn't block, as noted by many a naysayer—increased to gale force and were accompanied by sleet and rain. With the waves coming in a straight line from that horizon, the Furness Withy steamer *Graciana*, arriving to load apples, was unable to get into the harbour for fear of being thrashed about by the heavy seas and getting pushed ashore or ending up on one of the reefs that lie off Halifax. The captain was forced to claw his way back out to sea and ride out the storm. It was a trying night, but the ship survived; when it entered the harbour in the morning and the captain beheld the destruction, he would know he had made the right decision.

The seas were rolling in and being caught by the exposed quay at the outer end, then were flung along the wall into the basin with disastrous effect. Foley Brothers' tug *Lord Roberts* had earlier set out for Eastern Passage to inspect the company's dredge. Halfway across the harbour, the seas boarded the tug with such frequency that the skipper, fearing his boat would swamp, turned around and began a desperate run to get back to the Ocean Terminals before the water doused the engine room fires and put the pumps out of action. It arrived half full of water and came crashing in alongside a barge moored to the dock, smashing its deckhouse in, while the captain and crew of six jumped onto the barge just in time to see their tug go down in fifteen metres of water. Meanwhile, a heavily loaded barge carrying sand and cement—the one that serviced the diving bell, no doubt—also filled with water and sank near the *Lord Roberts.*

The ship tied to the outer berth was unhampered by the flotilla of barges that had collected beside the other steamer and suffered practically no damage, but the ship at the inner berth, tied to a feeble mooring, protected by the makeshift fenders, and crowded by the contractor's vessels, suffered a violent surge that slammed the ship against the dock. The starboard plates of the steamer were pushed in, and rivets sprung for twenty feet. The heavy granite blocks at the top of the wall cracked and were loosened by the pounding of the steamer. They disappeared overboard.

All of this spelled more unscheduled work for Foley et al. to refloat their barge and tug, replace the lost materials, and repair their just-completed work to the dock.

The storm caused damage throughout the harbour and the city. Roofs blew off buildings; chimneys, trees, and telephone poles were knocked down and windows were blown in. The tug *Boonton* sank near Pier 2, and the schooner *Pink* had a hole punched in its side; it sank after its mooring line snapped and the stern swung into the submerged *Boonton*. The schooner *Gladys and Lillian*, tied at the south side of Neville's Wharf, broke its lines and drove its bowsprit, the long timber that juts forward from a schooner's bow, into the office building of Robin, Jones, and Whitman, punching a large hole into the building's side.[85]

A year later, G. A. McLeod, comptroller for Foley et al., was set to defend the docks to the Nova Scotia Society of Engineers. "Their true worth," he argued, "will only be known when they are in operation as a completed whole...."[86] Indeed. McLeod didn't get to deliver his speech, though, because of a scheduling problem. He was set to speak on Thursday December 6, 1917—the day that began with the 9:04 A.M. Halifax Explosion.

That defining event in Halifax history occurred when a French ammunition ship, the *Mont Blanc*, loaded with flammables and explosives—a bad combination—collided with the SS *Imo* and caught fire. Officers and crew immediately abandoned the ship, which drifted to Richmond Terminals Pier 6 and grounded. After burning for twenty minutes, it exploded, killing some two thousand, injuring nine thousand and leaving twenty-five thousand homeless. The North End of Halifax was wrecked, especially the railway infrastructure and docks. Crucial to the war effort, getting the trains and ships moving again was second only to finding and treating the injured.

CHAPTER 17

THE THIRD RAILWAY STATION

A "temporary" wooden railway station at South Terminal, built in the winter of 1918–19 to replace the shattered old North Depot, remained for ten years the shabby and unlovely gateway to the city.[87]

– Thomas Raddall, *Halifax: Warden of the North*

ABOUT SEVENTY-FIVE RAILWAY WORKERS WERE DEAD AND MANY MORE WERE UNABLE TO REPORT TO WORK, while hundreds of railway cars were out of service, destroyed, or damaged. The Richmond Depot was completely smashed, much of the roof of the North Street Station was down on the tracks, and Deepwater was in chaos.[88] The unfinished Ocean Terminals had to fill the gap, worsening the disruption already caused by the explosion. Trains were immediately diverted in that direction, while two cranes were moved over to clear the way to the North Street Station. Railway staff occupied the buildings used by the construction engineers; doctors, nurses, and other staff brought in from elsewhere were billeted in sleeping cars heated by locomotives' fires.

Even though the rails of the Ocean Terminals Railway had only been used for construction trains, and the terminals were without any proper means for loading and unloading freight and lacked any passenger accommodation, it was possible to get relief trains to the heart of the city. The tracks had been finished for almost a year but Cook and Wheaton had been busy constructing the bridges over the cut through 1917 so they weren't useable. That all had to stop; on the day after the explosion the first regular trains departed Halifax for Montréal from the Ocean Terminals.[89] The first relief trains arrived within hours of the explosion from Truro, Kentville, New Glasgow, Amherst, Pictou, then from Moncton and Saint John. In the first six days at least twenty trains came, with five arriving from Montréal, four from Moncton, and others from Ottawa, Toronto, Bangor, Boston, New York, and Providence.[90]

By 6:00 P.M. on Saturday, December 8, the first passenger train pulled out. Full train service was restored from the North Street Station on the 10th after a superhuman effort by many people, including those working on the Ocean Terminals project. Rebuilding Richmond Terminals at that point was impractical. Instead, new sheds—numbers 25 and 28—were erected on Ocean Terminals Pier A. Number 25 was 181 metres long by 27 metres wide, and number 28 was 168 metres long by 27 metres wide. By January 18, foundations and framing for the sheds were completed and they would soon be ready for filling up. But having the docks and tracks in place did not mean the terminals were ready for action. Cargo, people, and mail could not go directly from a ship and onto a train. Goods needed a storage area—transit sheds—where the boxes, barrels, and crates could wait to be loaded into boxcars for movement to their final destinations. In some cases, the transition time from ship to train could be significant. Without the transit sheds, it would not be possible.

The railways incurred significant staff and equipment losses. CGR lost fifty-five workers and ten retirees. Almost 500 cars were damaged or destroyed, including 374 freight cars consisting of 139 from CGR, 96 from Canadian Pacific, 43 from Grand Trunk, 10 from New York Central, and 82 from other railways. Four cars could not be accounted for as they had been blown into the harbour and no records could be found. Thirty-seven of the freight cars were completely destroyed. A further 38 lost their tops, but they could be converted to flat- or pulpwood cars. The remaining 299 freight cars could be repaired.[91]

The explosion produced the biggest loss of life in an avoidable disaster in Canadian history, profoundly affecting the city. The rebuilding effort was massive, and from the beginning council knew they would need their steadfast city engineer, Major FWW Doane of the Halifax Rifles. On December 11, in their first meeting following the December 6 event, the Board of Control voted on whether to recall the major.

Most felt they should try to carry on without such a drastic move, so they deferred for the time being. A month later, they were forced to pass a resolution to see if they could get him back from Europe. Feelers went out to the military authorities and to FWW himself, asking if he was willing to return. It was unusual for an uninjured soldier who had not finished his tour to come home while the war was still raging. Matters came to a head in March when the military asked for permission to put up buildings on the Common and around the Citadel. The city was accommodating, but while they were working out the details, military buildings started going up and fences were erected, blocking long-standing shortcuts across the Common that people had used for generations.

That did it. They needed FWW; nobody else would do. It wasn't only the railways that were pushing the city around. By April 30, it was simply a matter of when he would arrive. On that day, council was meeting about problems with the water system and hoping out loud that he would soon appear. It took until July 11, 1918, when he was welcomed home exactly four months before the Armistice was declared on November 11, 1918.

On March 21, 1918, the Department of Railways and Canals issued a tender for the continued development of the Ocean Terminals. It included transit sheds for Piers 21 and 22 to be located not far from where the gas plant had stood since 1843. The plant—located where Peace and Friendship Park now stands—was too big to move, so it was demolished and rebuilt at Lower Water and Morris Streets, where it operated until December 1, 1952. Today, that site is a parking lot. Along with roadwork and water and sewage systems, the tender called for buildings that included the car-cleaning shop (a must for passenger cars), an icehouse, and, notably, a new passenger station—but not the fancy one that the 1912 announcement had promised. A temporary one was all that limited time and money would allow. In the middle of 1916, the railway had issued tenders for the new railway station, but the offers would cost more than the government felt it could afford so they backtracked for the time being. Then the explosion happened, and a station was absolutely necessary. In March they issued a tender due April 13, 1918, for a temporary station. On May 17, 1918, the tender went to the construction firm of Merrison and Downing for $88,772. Unlike its predecessors, the entrance to this station was a five-minute walk from Hollis Street, a main downtown thoroughfare.

This station would be the third, but not the last, in the exasperating history of rail service to Halifax.

On December 21, 1918, five and a half years after the project broke ground and sixty years after the railway had arrived in Halifax, the last passenger train, the Saint John night express, arrived at the North Street Station, which had been cobbled together to get the travelling public to this day. The next day, the new station at the Ocean Terminals opened for business. By then the ICR had ceased to exist. It had been merged with other money-losing railways the federal government had been obliged to take over. They all came under the umbrella of the CGR—more a term than a company. The company by then was

Looking south toward the gas plant from the location of the Nova Scotian Hotel, with Point Pleasant Park and the breakwater in the distance, April 1915. For 110 years, coal gas was manufactured and used in Halifax for lighting, heating, and cooking. [Halifax Municipal Archives CR6-122.75]

the CNR, incorporated by the federal government on December 20, 1918—the day before the new station opened. On January 20, 1923, the CNR assumed the management and operation of all the railway assets owned by the federal government. It would continue for decades to absorb others.

The station announcement in the newspaper was awkward: "The Terminal is of a temporary character"[92]—as though pairing "temporary" with "character" would somehow give the building prestige, but this plain wooden structure, built in less than seven months, could not match what the North Street Station had been. There were no celebrations or speeches for the crowd, estimated in the thousands, that turned out for the occasion. It was a big event despite the circumstances. During the previous five and a half years, they must have despaired that this day would ever come. But better times were ahead. The war had finally ended six weeks earlier, and Christmas was just days away.

The first train to leave the new temporary station departed at 3:00 P.M. on December 22. It was the Maritime Express to Montréal. Many dignitaries, including Board of Trade President Fred Pearson, were aboard for the ride, carried in the private car of CNR Superintendent J. T. Hallisey, attached to the end of the train. The Maritime Express was headed to Montréal, but the superintendent's car would be disconnected at the next station. The brand new Fairview station was at the point where the train exits the cut and the new route connects with the main line. Alongside was a new oceanside marshalling yard that had been built with rock and gravel taken from the north end of the railway cut and deposited into the southwest corner of the Bedford Basin, infilling out to a depth of eight to ten metres.

In this area, the ICR had come under bitter criticism in April 1914, after Lillian Bayer, a twenty-four-year-old Dalhousie University student, had been run over and killed after getting off the train in the dark. Her aunt had the traumatic experience of finding her body on the track while searching for her in the middle of the night when she did not return as scheduled. Bayer was to graduate in a matter of days and was found carrying her new graduation gown in her arms. The tracks run by the Bedford Basin, and the area was in the process of being infilled. Investigators concluded that she was on the water side of the tracks and had been walking in the dark on a narrow strip of land between the stopped train and the large boulders waiting to be pushed overboard. When the train moved it must have startled her and she fell under the wheels.

The inquiry report noted:

> The said Lillian Bayer came to her death by falling under the wheels of train No. 9 on the evening of April 8th, 1914, at Rockingham Station. We are further of the opinion that this calamity would not have occurred had the Intercolonial Railway authorities provided proper and adequate facilities such as platform extension, lighting and stricter attention to their duty on the part of the railway employees.[93]

The dignitaries' ride back from Fairview to the new station was described by *The Halifax Herald*—drearily supportive to the end—which seized the opportunity to take a swat at the sights to be seen on the old route to the North Street Station.

> It is a picturesque run from Fairview, the steep walls of rock on either side, the sixteen beautiful bridges, the glimpse at the Arm and the pretty country traversed contrasting strongly with the tumble-down buildings, the devastated district and the squalor of Africville, which met the eye on the old line from Fairview in.[94]

Africville was an underserviced Black community. The rail line ran through this neighbourhood.

⌗⌗⌗⌗⌗⌗⌗⌗

The North Street Station was handed over to the Department of Militia and Defence to be used for making up and equipping troop and hospital trains. Given that the war had just ended there would be many thousands of soldiers, nurses, and other people arriving from Europe and bound for points across Canada. Freight would continue to be handled at the Richmond Yards for the time being.

In the Rockingham area in 1918, cars were getting shunted to sidings and prepared for service. Passenger cars would be cleaned and heated for oncoming travellers. The water of the basin nearby was a convenient place for the custodians to dump the trash thereby collected, which they did for years, if not decades, judging by what's down there. In that area I have done many dozens of happy dives and made some worthwhile additions to my antique bottle and chinaware collections. I've found interesting milk, soda pop, and medicine bottles from unlikely places like Sudbury and Gloucester. The most unusual find is a pop bottle from the Panama Railway. I don't know how that one found its way to Halifax. It would definitely have needed to make a few connections, but it arrived only to be unceremoniously dumped into the harbour.

The evidence that all this detritus came from the trains is to be found in the countless number of damaged dishes from the CNR—cups with missing handles, plates with dings on the rim, pieces of milk jugs and broken bowls from different periods in CNR history. There are fields of coal ash from steam locomotives and there is a surprising amount of coal, some pieces the size of a basketball.

CHAPTER 18

THE ROCKY ROAD TO PIER 21

Problems of economic recovery and social readjustments; problems of rehabilitating the nation's commerce; problems of sustaining the nation's credit and financial structure, all conspired to hinder resumption of the interrupted program of port building.[95]

– J. S. Scott, Author

IN LATE AUGUST 1916, ENGINEER ARTHUR BROWN TOLD THE UNION OF NOVA SCOTIA MUNICIPALITIES, "THE main line work...is now practically finished and grading, ditching and trimming of slopes are proceeding rapidly. Preparations are being made to begin track laying and ballasting and in a few weeks time trains will be coming into the terminals over permanent track."[96] But the project was supposed to be finished. Their deadline for completion had been July 1, 1915. On June 10 they came looking for an extension to January 1, 1916. When that date arrived, they had already requested another extension to October 1, 1916. They rumbled past that one and got another deadline of September 1, 1917. Maritime Bridge Company, with contracts for the Chebucto Road and Fairview overpasses—where the tracks would go over the road instead of under—had also extended to December 31, 1917. And Foley et al. were doing no better; they had extended their deadline to June 1, 1918.

You would think that the arrival of a ship tying up on official business at an Ocean Terminals berth would herald the completion of the project, but close to a dozen years would pass between the arrival of the cargo ship SS *Sheba* in November 1916 and the opening of the immigration quarters at Pier 21, and even more time would pass before the union station and railway hotel would be standing. A lot had been accomplished but the promises of 1912 were far from delivered. Even though the idea of a new immigration facility along the huge modern quay with indoor access to a nearby train was exciting, there was no rush because Pier 2 was already getting the job done. The war, and then rebuilding after the explosion, got all the attention and money.

Given the location, the conditions, the tools, and the events that befell the contractors, it's remarkable that they actually got it finished. Halifax existed for the harbour and the harbour existed for the navies and the convoys. Everything else had to stay out of the way. The project, however, was to some extent *in* the way. The minesweepers patrolling the harbour approaches were kept in the Northwest Arm, coming and going daily, crossing the same space as the barges of stone from the quarries. Those same barges then had to be navigated around the Point Pleasant shoals, which forced them dangerously close to the traffic lanes. And the barges, cranes, cement mixers, dredges, and drilling rigs were on the water at the entrance to the harbour, leaving their operators constantly on edge.

As the war picked up, Foley et al. was often called upon to divert cranes to assist in moving and removing heavy guns from ships. After 1916, completed berths got put to work for active shipping, even though they were in the middle of a construction zone. The traffic was such that one of the Ocean Terminals basins was available for construction work for less than a third of the time during the whole of 1917.[97] Then, the explosion knocked out all the marine infrastructure at Richmond Terminals and a lot of Deepwater. Anything usable at Ocean Terminals got pressed into service, leading to dangerous situations. On February 4, 1918, Louis Pare of Quebec was unloading a carload of pine logs at Pier A. He cut the posts holding them in but the last one broke and the logs started tumbling off the car. He leapt aside but caught his heel in a track and fell backward. The logs came down on top of him, killing him instantly.

On March 9, 1918, Foley et al.'s tugs were needed in the salvage of the SS *Saranac*, a steamship belonging to the United States Shipping

Cook and Wheaton justified their first request for an extension to the schedule after confronting the vast amount of rock that had to be removed near Tower Road. The existing bridge crosses at this point. In this image, workers are preparing explosives in June 1916. [Halifax Municipal Archives, MacLauchlan photo (CR6-122.32)]

Board that had run aground on McNabs Island in the blizzard the day after the explosion. Such situations became more common.

Wartime labour conditions also limited the supply of workers and increased the demands being made on them at a time when there were lots of other employment opportunities. In mid-1916, a recruiter went around the works promising better employment terms on another project, resulting in an exodus of sixty-five labourers, and causing unrest among those remaining. Labour shortages also drove up wages, increasing the costs for the contractors by more than $1 million.[98] Recouping these costs was a major challenge. In 1921 the contractors sought additional compensation of over $500,000 from the

Department of Railways and Canals for expenses caused by the war and the explosion that led to use of the Ocean Terminals before the work was complete. The hard-pressed federal government rejected the claim.[99]

One way to recoup costs was by moonlighting. In the spring of 1917, Cook and Wheaton contracted with the city to build a bridge over a brook running into the Northwest Arm at the place where the Armdale Roundabout is today. In another case, the city needed a trunk sewer line built from Oakland Road to Chain Rock at Point Pleasant. Cook and Wheaton were in the neighbourhood with the required equipment, and they were familiar with the terrain. Considering the hard time the federal government gave the contractors when they asked for additional funds to cover unpleasant surprises, it must have been a pleasant surprise for Cook and Wheaton when they presented

Steam-operated drilling rigs widening the cut in the fall of 1914. The Dartmouth shore is in the background. [Tom Lynskey collection]

the city with a change order for $15,000 to cover additional work in building the sewer and it was accepted and paid without a lot of drama.

After the explosion, there was so much new work available that Cook and Wheaton advertised: "Since the disaster we have been assigned considerable work which will keep us busy during the winter months and give steady employment to all carpenters and laborers who wish to apply for work."[100] In less than a month after the explosion, they were looking to expand their seven hundred workers with an additional four hundred for CGR work. Two large temporary sheds were needed at Pier A, and Piers 3 and 4 at Deepwater required significant work. The Richmond Yard, ground zero for the explosion, had to be rebuilt, along with the dockyard next door.

Foley et al. finally finished their contracted work over the summer of 1919, two years after their original deadline. That fall, the Dominion Bridge Company erected the steel framing for the transit sheds at the passenger landing pier. Wartime constraints on steel production and the priority for rebuilding the city following the explosion severely limited the supply and quality of materials, meaning that the buildings lacked the flair and elegance that the original designs had specified.

At the end of 1919, Foley et al.'s resident engineer, Arthur Brown, with his contract completed, went to work for one of the subcontractors he had managed, Halifax firm J. P. Porter and Associates, on a project in Saint-Pierre, a French island south of Newfoundland. That was followed by another Canadian government contract similar to the Ocean Terminals—an addition to the Welland Canal on Lake Ontario, where he filled the role of engineering superintendent, returning to England in 1925. At age forty-four, and married with two daughters, he died from malaria in 1932 while working in Singapore.

Other major players in the Ocean Terminals enterprise were leaving. On July 1, 1920, under pressure from his doctors, Prime Minister Robert Borden announced his retirement from politics. In 1924, after thirty-three years, FWW retired as the city engineer. He spent the next eight years as a consulting engineer and then started a third career, which lasted twenty-six years, with Standard Paving, where he was still employed when he died in April 1958 at age ninety-four. He served on numerous boards, lectured at Dalhousie University, and received an honourary Doctor of Engineering degree. He even completed an exhaustive history of his regiment, the Halifax Rifles, and was promoted to lieutenant colonel. His stately house, built in 1898 and which he owned until 1955, still stands on Young Avenue. The owner was a survivor—and so is his house.

After the final push, the project languished. The sheds put in place during the war were only temporary wooden structures, reflecting the city itself with its rows of wooden buildings erected by the Halifax Relief Commission to house people who had lost their homes. No further contracts were awarded, and construction halted after 1919 as a postwar economic slowdown set in. Ship traffic at the port slowed as competition from American ports increased. In 1922, CNR proposed that the government allocate funds to at least complete the sheds that had been started, but the department refused. Some of the project's most enthusiastic supporters were passing. On June 2, 1923, Michael Dwyer died from kidney failure at age forty-seven. Samuel Brookfield died in August 1924. George Campbell died in 1927.

Where one would have expected a grand opening with flags and speeches, the Ocean Terminals project was an orphan, an impressive but unfinished accomplishment lacking funds and a champion to take it over the finish line. The issues that the Board of Trade griped about in 1912 and that they expected the Ocean Terminals development to address had, in some respects, not improved. Large events over which the city had no control—national economic fortunes, the war, the explosion, post-war deflation—slowed the city's growth to a halt. The optimistic projections behind the Ocean Terminals did not materialize. At the cost of a prime section of valuable real estate and fourteen acres of shoreline at Point Pleasant Park, Halifax was left instead with a large and permanent federal transportation complex—a cultural dead zone for people to whisk past on their way to the park.

Maritimers threw out the Conservative government that had started the Ocean Terminals project, put the city and its people through such a trial, and then lost interest. The federal Liberals didn't improve matters, so citizens went back to the Conservatives in 1925. The sun finally broke through as the federal government advised the CNR to make proposals for completion of the terminals. An announcement of renewed work followed. On November 17, 1925, CNR Vice-President J. E. Dalrymple and the Atlantic management team came to Halifax to commiserate with the council of the Board of Trade. They assured the members that work on the immigration sheds and other infrastructure was being resumed.

They also met with representatives of the large shipping firms to announce that grain shipments from Halifax would be increasing. As with mail and immigrants, Halifax had become the winter port for grain exports. It started in late January 1881 when the barque *Chili* loaded the first shipment of 38,500 bushels of wheat directly from railway boxcars that arrived from Detroit. The *Chili* was in Halifax to unload raw sugar that was bound for Montréal but could not be delivered because the St. Lawrence was frozen. The wheat needed a ship and the *Chili* was empty, so Captain Herd took the load and departed on January 28. More came after, and wheat soon turned into regular business for the port. Temporary facilities had to be built to load ships directly from the railway cars pending the construction of Halifax's first grain elevator, which went into operation the next year and was busy until it burned in 1895. M. E. Keefe and Co. built the replacement elevator at Deepwater, and it got demolished when the new elevator at Ocean Terminals was completed in October 1925.

That one cost $1 million and was lying empty, but with the new resolve to put the terminals to work it quickly proved to be inadequate. The initial forty-eight silos from 1924 were soon expanded, taking capacity to 2,200,000 bushels by 1934,[101] and in 1953 ninety-two more silos were added.[102] In the fall of 1964, business was booming and ships were forced to unload their grain onto the floors of cargo sheds because the 4,152,000-bushel elevator was packed full.[103] By 1967, it had become the biggest structure in the city; it now looms ominously above a residential neighbourhood.

The elevator's growth over the years mirrors the expansion of Canada's grain shipments. Today it has 365 silos and capacity for more than five million bushels. Very little wheat is exported from Halifax anymore but each autumn the bins are full, thanks to wood pellets and crops of Maritime-grown soybeans. Plenty of wheat is kept in reserve but it's consumed locally as P&H Milling next door provides flour for the bakeries of Atlantic Canada. The grain elevator's future is uncertain, however. Instead of meeting a need for which it was built, a lot of effort now goes into finding uses to which it can be put. It's a monster occupying very valuable land as the container terminal next door continues to expand at a time when more people are jamming onto the peninsula.

In February 1928 the Standard Construction Company of Halifax announced the completion of the new terminal buildings and were ready to have their work shown off. The first thing of note was a covered passageway leading from the immigration rooms at Pier 21 to the (temporary) train station. The new facilities included waiting rooms, some of which were private for larger families, baggage examination rooms, a canteen, dining room, and rest areas (complete with nursing

The M. E. Keefe Construction Company built the 160-foot-tall grain elevator at Pier 3 in 1899. It occupied the space below where the traffic circle was constructed on Barrington Street in 2024. Grain was stored in the lower section and the weighing and distribution machinery was in the upper part, called the cupola. [Notman Studio NS Archives 1983-310 number 100026]

areas for women and with attendants to look after other children). There were five detention rooms—two for men, two for women, and one for ships' crew that might need to be held. There was even a hospital with an operating room and apartments for doctors and nurses.[104]

It was steam heated, which was common in those days, but the steam heating in this case originated off-site at the Nova Scotia Tramways and Power Company's plant on Lower Water Street. There, the steam was used to drive generators to supply electricity to Halifax customers, but in this case the company was selling some of it to the terminal buildings. In congratulating themselves for their contribution to the new buildings, the power company advertised, "In these new buildings our gas will be used in the several modern kitchens for cooking and water heating. Our electricity will be used for the modern lighting equipment. Our gas coke was used for heating the huge kettles in which the mastic flooring was prepared."[105] As electricity continued to constitute a bigger part of their business, the company renamed itself Nova Scotia Light and Power, and in 1971 it became the Nova Scotia Power Corporation, under government ownership. Today it is just one arm of a private multinational energy corporation named Emera, headquartered in Halifax on land it has owned for close to a century and a half.

Immigration officials didn't rush to make use of the new site. They were happy where they were at Pier 2 and didn't want to leave. When, in late 1925, the CNR officially gave notice to the immigration department that a move was in the works, it warned that there was no choice because all transatlantic shipping would be landing at the new piers. The first group of immigrants to disembark at Pier 21 arrived on Friday March 8, 1928. Fifty-one passengers from Rotterdam, via Boulogne and Southampton, arrived on the Holland-America steamship *Nieuw Amsterdam*. The following day, more ships arrived. First was the *Oscar II* of the Scandinavian-American Line from Copenhagen and Oslo, landing 2 first-class and 121 third-class passengers. Next was Cunard's *Tuscania* followed by the Anchor-Donaldson Line's *Athenia*. In total, 709 were landed at Pier 21 on day two.[106]

CHAPTER 19

ALMOST THERE

We make this statement with a full knowledge of conditions, that if a new hotel is started in Halifax on the scale proposed, it will be reorganized or meet with failure within the next five years.[107]

– The Halifax Hotel and The Queen Hotel

THE PROJECT LAID OUT DURING THE 1912 LUNCHEON HAD STILL NOT DELIVERED ON ITS PROMISES. THE original plans showed that five and a half piers were to be built, the half one being the inner side of the breakwater. However, the contracts let in 1913 were for just one-and-a-half piers—and that's what was built. But that didn't stop mapmakers from showing what looks like six two-sided piers, which reflected what Frank Cochrane had originally presented to the Board of Trade. In a presentation to the Canadian Society of Civil Engineers in 1917, Arthur Brown stated, "The terminals consist of a passenger landing quay 2,006 feet long, five piers 1,250 feet long by an average of 350 feet, and a breakwater about 1,600 feet long, on the north side of which will be constructed later two steamship berths."[108] Not then, nor ever, were there five piers, nor four. It took until after 1955 before there were even three.

After 1925, when there was finally some impetus by the government of the day to finish what remained of the project and move it forward, the big items on everybody's wish list were the new railway hotel and the permanent Union Station. It was time for the Board of Trade to remobilize. In 1912, a rumour had circulated that a new hotel was planned for the corner of Spring Garden Road and South Park Street.

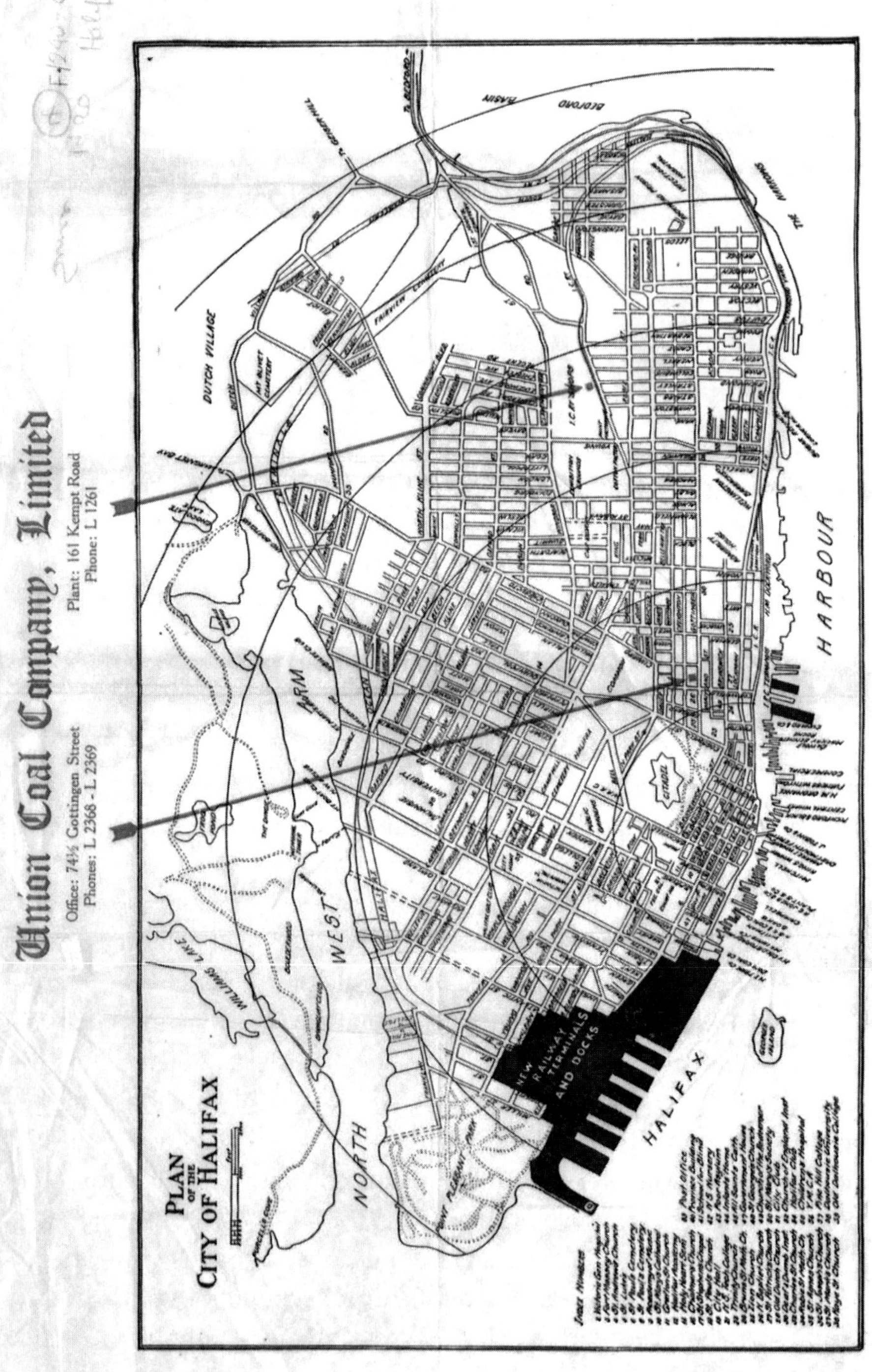

This 1916 map of Halifax depicts what looks like six two-sided piers plus a breakwater (the area in black at lower left), reflecting the plan Frank Cochrane had originally presented to the Board of Trade but was never actually implemented. [NS Archives Map Collection: V6 240 Halifax]

Hugh Silver, who had moved to 101 South Park Street after his Pleasant Street house, named Parkland, had been expropriated, led a campaign to turn that rumour into reality. Interest was high and investors were many. After the first week of July 1927, in just two days of selling, they had sold $100,000 in the stock of the Lord Nelson Hotel Company. By mid-October they were within $70,000 of their $1,170,000 goal. Silver had been energetically encouraging participation from both of Canada's national railways, Canadian National and Canadian Pacific. CP was interested but CN was sending mixed signals. Management was all aboard, but the federal government controlled the money.

When Canadian Pacific invested $350,000, the goal was met—and the CNR was left outside looking in. On October 15, Hugh Silver called for quotations. H. L. Stevens and Company won the tender. C. C. Moore and R. W. Millard arrived from Toronto to sign the construction contract. The sod-turning could only be on Trafalgar Day, October 21, to commemorate Lord Horatio Nelson's victory—at the cost of his life—over a combined French and Spanish fleet off Cape Trafalgar in 1805. In the presence of nearly a thousand people, Mayor J. B. Kenny turned the sod and work began. To the Board of Trade, getting CP into Halifax was a big win. They already owned the Dominion Atlantic Railway, headquartered in Kentville and servicing the Annapolis Valley. It was logical that more Canadian Pacific ships would be calling at Halifax. Local investors in the new hotel included shipping companies Furness Withy & Co. Ltd., Farquhar and Company, Pickford & Black, and G. S. Campbell & Company, all shipowners.

But it wasn't the railway hotel everybody had been longing for and CNR President Sir Henry Thornton knew it. On April 14 he declared that the CNR would immediately begin construction of a hotel at the Ocean Terminals. He was pre-empting his political masters, the federal government, prompting the *Herald* to declare, "The see-sawing manoeuvres between the C.N.R. and the federal government in reference to cooperation or equipping Halifax with a C.N.R. hotel are liable, if continued, to make the people dizzy."[109] On October 18, Sir Henry headed to Halifax with three vice-presidents, the railway's chief engineer, and an architect in tow. They chose a site for a new CNR hotel and station near the Ocean Terminals and announced that construction would begin immediately—fast-tracked for completion during the winter months.

Heads were spinning. The two leading hotels of the day, The Halifax and The Queen, were in shock. First the Lord Nelson and now this! Though they despised one another, and their employees were known to engage in an occasional brawl, the times called for desperate measures. A long, whiny ad showed up in the papers, complaining about how there was not enough business for such an infusion of new capacity.

Nobody noticed. The *Chronicle*'s front-page story on October 21 announced that the Lord Nelson Company and CN Hotels were starting construction that day. For the Lord Nelson's builders, it was full steam ahead, but at the CNR site there was a problem even getting up steam. They did some excavating and put in part of a foundation, and then everything got sidetracked yet again. Months passed. Finally, on March 26, 1928, light appeared at the end of the tunnel as the government finally came up with the money—$1,250,000 for a new railway station and hotel at Halifax. Foundation Maritime Limited got the contract on August 7, 1928.

Six months later, on October 23, 1928, the Lord Nelson opened, a year almost to the day after construction began. More than 350 attended a grand ball, and the next evening the Board of Trade hosted a banquet for 400 people. The opening ad stressed its "absolutely fireproof" construction. Hotel fires had historically been big disasters because the buildings were usually wooden and held a lot of people. On the horizon was a reminder of its importance when The Queen Hotel burned on March 2, 1939, resulting in twenty-eight deaths.

The Lord Nelson Hotel featured an interesting novelty—a radio broadcasting studio on the top floor. Maritime Broadcasting Limited had brought radio to Nova Scotia with radio station CHNS in 1926, broadcasting from the Carleton Hotel with a 100-watt transmitter. The Lord Nelson's design had included a studio equipped with a 500-watt transmitter, ready for CHNS to move into.

Six months after his hotel project ran off the rails, Sir Henry Thornton reappeared and this time he was firmly on track. Opening day was June 23, 1930, during a period of feverish hotel building for the CNR, with eight hotels up across the country and three more under

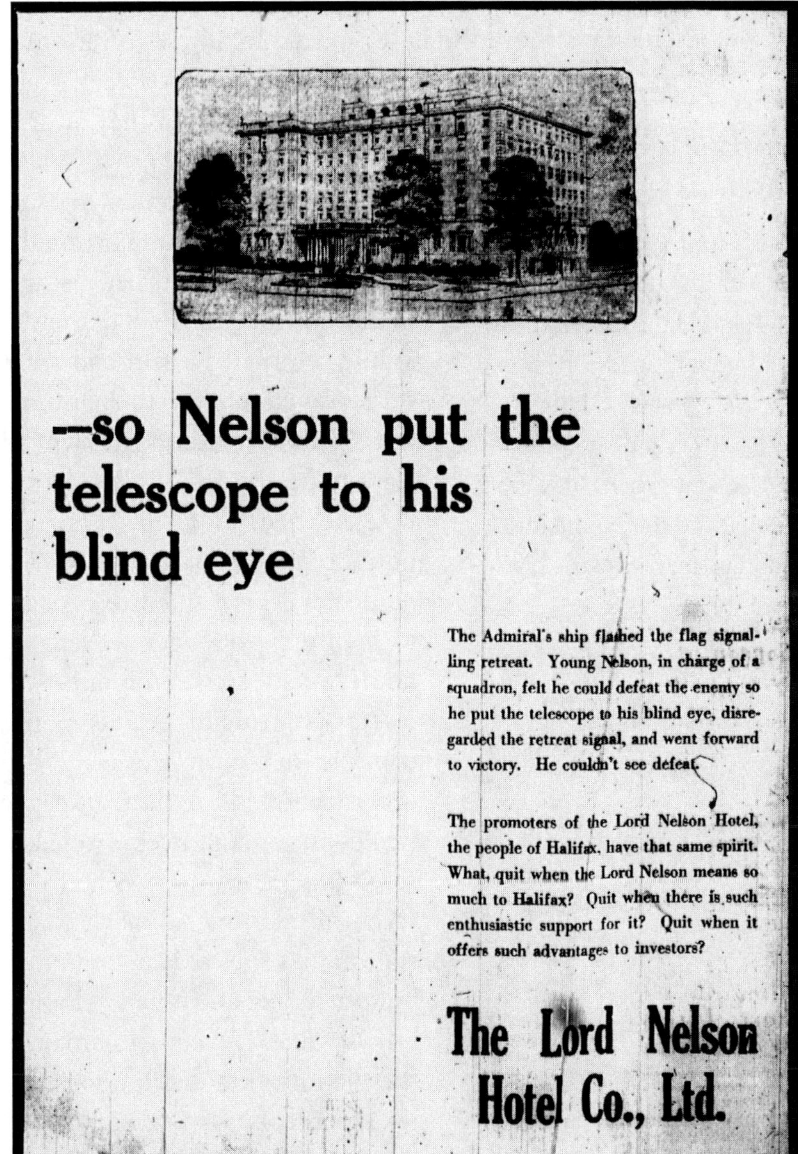

This advertisement for the Lord Nelson Hotel appeared in The Halifax Herald *on July 18, 1927.*

construction. As the ninth to open, the Nova Scotian Hotel entered the distinguished company of inns like the Château Laurier and Jasper Park Lodge. The day before the hotel started taking reservations, Sir Henry invited the people of Halifax to check it out—and they swarmed the place!

From *The Halifax Herald*, June 24, 1930:

Thousands upon thousands of visitors strolled through the spacious halls and admired the luxurious appointments of the Nova Scotian, latest addition to the C.N.R.'s chain of hotels across Canada, when it was thrown open to the public for inspection yesterday.

From the time the doors were opened in the morning, throngs of the interested and the curious examined the hotel from the rotunda to the radio room on the roof. During the afternoon every hall was packed, and the stairs were almost impassable. And when attendants cleared the building at 9 o'clock last evening, crowds still sought admittance.[117]

The CNR's visionary president liked to win, and even in something as obscure as radio broadcasting he managed to better the competition. While the Lord Nelson had a radio station as a tenant in the penthouse, the CNR was operating its own radio station in the penthouse of their hotel. When Sir Henry first heard of radio broadcasting to the masses, he decided he wanted to broadcast to his train passengers. There were no networks, so he built one—CNR Radio—starting in 1925. Passengers could sit in a parlour car and listen on earphones or horn speakers while an operator controlled the receiving sets to maintain the reception. To overcome the lack of stations, a series of transmitters was built at cities and towns along the railway line. Of course, anyone in the vicinity of a station could pick up the broadcasts so the audience extended beyond train passengers to the public at large. By the early 1930s, there was pressure to provide a public broadcasting system, and in 1933 the federal government took over CNR Radio as the foundation for the Canadian Broadcasting Corporation.

The Lord Nelson had created a sensation, but the *real* railway hotel was the one the people had been yearning for because it included the

The completed cold storage plant in 1931 with the unfinished Pier B—which became 1A—in the foreground. Across the tracks stands the grain elevator, which was destined to grow much larger over the decades. [McCully NS Archives 2012-010/003 no. 11, negative 187]

long-awaited Union Station. The temporary station, what the *Herald* called, "the unsightly shack which was allowed to remain at the South End Terminals ever since the war" was finally gone.[110] Travellers arriving by ship or train could get to the hotel without having to venture outdoors by simply passing through a doorway—a huge deal in 1930s Halifax.

The arrival of the hotel and station were the last big pieces of what Cowie had envisioned, but additions to the site would continue. Work had begun on the second pier, Pier B, but it was still unfinished when construction of the Nova Scotia Public Cold Storage Terminals began in October 1928. This cold storage plant was needed to provide storage for frozen products arriving or leaving.

Completed in 1930, the plant stood for years on the infilled shore in front of the unfinished Pier B, delaying that pier's development past the state in which the contractors had left it after the Halifax Explosion. By the spring of 1930, a third pier, this one also dubbed Pier B, started construction, with J. P. Porter and Sons dredging for its foundations south of the partially finished one. The 381-metre–long by 91.5-metre–wide wharf was completed in 1932. But it, too, got delayed, affected by the Depression, and there was no money for sheds. The naked dock sat idle like the original unfinished Pier B next to it. Then, on February 14, 1934, the government issued a contract for five transit sheds to extend along the whole length of the new Pier B, along with railway tracks on each side. Prime Minister R. B. Bennett, a Dalhousie University graduate, finally opened that pier on December 10, 1934. The unfinished one lingered between A and B for another quarter century and was finished between 1955 and 1960. It ended up being called Pier A1 and was the final component of Cowie's vision to be completed.

That closed the book on Frederick Cowie's inspiration, but it is not the end of the story. Big things still lay ahead.

CHAPTER 20

CASTING A LONG SHADOW

This port does not belong to Halifax. It does not belong to Nova Scotia. It belongs to Canada, built by the nation for the nation.[111]

– J. L. Hetherington, Chairman, Halifax Harbour Commission

NOT A SOUL WAS AROUND ON THE FROSTY SUNDAY AFTERNOON IN THE MID-1990S WHEN MY BUDDY AND I arrived at Pier 20, put on our dive gear, and slipped into the -1°C water where Foley et al. had laid the first concrete block in 1915. There were no ships tied up and there was no other boat traffic to be seen, just the long quay stretching more than half a kilometre. For the first time, I saw those neat granite blocks as we descended, all lined up perfectly, but not appreciating what an undertaking their construction had entailed. I picked up my first piece of chinaware from a Cunard ship, a teacup bearing what now is a familiar logo—a lion holding a globe—but at the time I didn't recognize it.

That cup was the only thing picked up on the dive because we were not familiar with the distinct nature of the area. Because the water is not particularly deep, the huge propellers on the ships that tie up there can affect the bottom. Modern cruise ships are very manoeuvrable because their propellers, called azipods, can pivot through 360 degrees which, when used with their bow thrusters, gives them the ability to even move sideways. When they push out from the dock, those propellers throw a lot of water against that granite wall. It deflects down and violently strikes the bottom, stirring up enormous amounts of mud and debris, including bottles, crockery, and chinaware. The bottom of most of Halifax Harbour is covered in dunes of drab, grey silt. The bottom below Piers 20, 21, and 22 looks like a bomb was dropped there—appropriate, considering the millions of dollars of dynamite that was set off a century before.

Over the years our dive group recovered fine collections of dishes from famous shipping lines like Cunard, White Star, Canadian Pacific, and others. Some of it is on display at the Canadian Museum of Immigration at Pier 21 topside. China from a ship finds its way to the bottom in two ways. First, in the days when they dumped the garbage overboard, it often included a bowl or plate that was scratched or dinged and no longer suitable for tableware. Second, an unblemished item would sometimes go over the side when somebody finished a coffee or snack on deck and didn't bother to return the china. Those are the ones we prefer because they're in mint condition, but we'll take the others as well. Every milk bottle or soup bowl ever made is somewhere, the most likely places being landfills and the ocean. The amount of debris that has gone and continues to go into the ocean is staggering. Critters like crabs usually gobble up anything organic, but if it's more durable it disappears into the mud. It may migrate down for decades until some fast-moving water comes along and flings it to a new place, where it begins to slowly sink again—unless a diver gets to experience a moment of joy. It's a matter of being in the right place at the right time.

A lot has happened since that important luncheon at The Halifax in 1912, when the city's voices of capitalism rose in harmony to extol the virtues of the minister of Railways and Canals. In 1930, the Nova Scotian Hotel replaced The Halifax, which had stood on the corner of Hollis and Salter Streets since 1841, as the city's premium venue for the well-heeled to lay their heads. Appropriately, the Nova Scotian Hotel became a part of the project they were celebrating and still sits in the northwest corner of the development with the rear parking lot bordering on infilled land put in place by the contractors.

If the windows of The Halifax had been open that day, those working at the waterfront might have heard the singing, but they would not have been able to stop and join in. They were too busy. The waterfront was abuzz with activity. Directly behind the hotel, employees at G. S. Campbell's docks were loading passengers on one of the Red Cross Line's ships, the *Stephano* or the *Florizel*, bound for New York or St. John's. Up the street, Michael Dwyer's employees would have been unloading tea from a vessel tied up alongside. Farther along, at Pickford & Black's wharves, a load of coconuts and oranges was coming ashore from one of W. A. Black's steamships just back from the Caribbean. Their bosses were busy too, revelling in the good times to come.

Little had Michael Dwyer imagined the impact the project would have on his own home. Nor had George Campbell expected to be wondering if a rock was going to come down through his roof. FWW was probably oblivious to the revelry, busy at his desk with his head down, carefully penning his latest report to the mayor on the subject of street lighting or road widening or water purity. He had no idea what lay ahead—fighting with James McGregor and Andrew Wheaton at home and the enemy abroad. Losing a son.

What they were singing about would bring changes to Halifax that some did not want, but which had to come if Halifax were to achieve its potential as a world-class commercial port. Nobody expected it to be so hard—and to have the war and the explosion occur at the same time only demonstrates their resolve. After the first frustrating years, a long period of change—changes in transportation, changes in technology, and changes in leisure activities—lay ahead, and the Ocean Terminals development would come just in time for Halifax to move along with it.

Tremendous strides in technology had been taking place in 1912. *Titanic*, the most famous ship ever built had sunk just six months before, essentially because the technology to propel it had outpaced the technology to control it. Even though the Halifax waterfront was the epicentre of commerce, like all such waterfronts in ports the world over, it was showing its age. Sail-powered schooners tied up there. Their days, like the wharves that harboured them, were also numbered. Vessels like the *Titanic*'s sister ship, *Olympic*, were regulars in Halifax.

They sailed past the waterfront and tied up at Deepwater, which was soon eclipsed by the Ocean Terminals, where the ships arrived, tarried briefly, and departed with ease.

Many ports did not recover from the changes that were occurring in shipping; those that did grew bigger and richer. The original Halifax waterfront's days as a bustling centre of shipping and commerce were numbered. It had been excellent when it served only the city and surrounding area but the need for much greater capacity was dawning—and with that need came opportunity. Bigger, faster, and stronger ships filled the need to carry more people, more mail, and more freight faster and farther. Those ships disgorged thousands of people at a time who needed to be processed and, more importantly, who needed seats or sleepers on a train to get them to far-flung destinations on their new continent. Trains still had a lot of development in their futures. Ocean Terminals served all of the city's railway needs, especially during the Second World War.

But things change and the Ocean Terminals had to change. Automobiles were a novelty in 1912, but they turned out to be a fitting competitor to the train. The highway system was the death knell for the small railway stations. It also replaced a lot of tracks, and a lot of passenger trains got replaced with cars, trucks, buses, and airplanes. Now the long-distance passenger trains run by Via Rail cater mainly to railway buffs and those averse to flying. In Canada, such trains are few.

The story of the fracas between Halifax and Saint John to host ships carrying the nation's mail sounds quaint today. But when Major J. H. Tudhope visited Halifax in his Fairchild monoplane on March 3, 1928, to scout out sites for an airport that would enable an air mail service between Halifax and Montréal, it marked the beginning of the end for seaborne mail. Many recall writing "Via Air Mail" on the outside of an envelope and later buying special lightweight airmail envelopes. That passed too, as all such mail has become snail mail compared to email, throwing postal services into the red.

With the coming of air travel, immigration into Halifax declined, dropping from nearly 26,000 in 1959 to less than 1,200 in 1970. Aircraft took away all the passenger liner traffic. The immigration office at Pier 21 closed as transatlantic passenger ship visits came to a trickle and then stopped. Ninety years of immigration into Halifax by sea ended with the closure of Pier 21 in March 1971. A museum was eventually built at the location to commemorate the many new Canadians who had come through there over forty-three years. It opened in 1999. Unfortunately, the forty-seven years of immigration through the Deep Water Terminus has been all but forgotten.

Halifax's railways needed to be rationalized, as well. In addition to the tracks through the railway cut, the original tracks from a century ago were still around, running from downtown at Nora Bernard Street north and around the peninsula all the way to Young Street, with spur lines running to businesses in the north end. Those tracks were still using the Deep Water Terminus, which the Ocean Terminals was supposed to replace.

An aerial view of the Deep Water Terminus, Piers 2 and 3, ca. 1960. [NS ARCHIVES PHOTOGRAPHIC COLLECTION]

The Ocean Terminals location was thick with tracks. In 1960 there were nine sets running under the Young Avenue bridge and six under Tower Road, indicating that the shunting of cars had been penetrating well into the neighbourhood. Eight sets of tracks ran onto Pier A alone, five ran onto Pier A1, and six ran out on Pier B. A visitor to the area today might wonder why there is so much empty space in the yard, but in 1960 it was packed in. At that time, more than eighty sets of tracks ran through the yard between the passenger station and Pier B.

The big change, though, as with sail to steam, has come with the movement of freight. The crowds of stevedores guiding slings of boxes into and out of ships' holds are long gone. The ships were big for the time, but by today's standards they were tiny. That was why the Ocean Terminals was designed with so many berths. Shipping required a lot of ships, and the Ocean Terminals project was expected to handle close to three dozen at a time. That never came to pass because only half the intended number of piers ever got built. By the time the government came around to thinking about it, the slings were gone, the stevedores were gone, and the ships had grown out of all proportion to what was around in 1912.

In the 1960s the Ocean Terminals were at a turning point. Study after study seemed unable to define what was to be done with the space that had caused so much disruption to construct. Consultants lined up to state the obvious. One report, by Murray V. Jones and Associates, was particularly critical of the Ocean Terminals location. Surrounded by parks and houses, there was no space to expand and no room to accommodate industry. There were much better places in the harbour in which to invest money, they said.

Really? It seemed like 1912 all over again.

Instead of starting yet again, as some studies were advocating, it made more sense to repurpose the existing site that had taken such toil to build. If it had been the best place in 1912, it could still be the best place going forward. Dispensing with what remained of the Deep Water Terminus was long overdue, down by then to just Piers 2 and 3. Why not expand at the Ocean Terminals instead of abandoning it?

There was space inside the breakwater that had been earmarked for the other finger piers that had never been built. At the southern end,

Above: The view in 2025 looking east toward Halifax Harbour from the Young Avenue rail bridge. Below: The view looking west from the Young Avenue bridge; the Tower Road bridge is visible in the distance. [CONTRIBUTED]

Infilling for the container terminal south of the Ocean Terminals ca. 1969. This image shows Piers B, A1, and part of A, as well as the Royal Canadian Navy jetty. The future site of the container terminal has been cleared and is ready for construction. Point Pleasant Park is on the right of the image. [HALIFAX MUNICIPAL ARCHIVES 101-80C-1-6-31]

between Pier B and the breakwater, was a large piece of shoreline that was ideal for a container terminal for all the reasons it had been ideal for new piers in 1912. The navy's Seaward Defence Base, which docked its first vessel, a US Coast Guard cutter up from Marblehead, MA, in 1953, occupied the space along with the Royal Nova Scotia Yacht Squadron.[112] In July 1968, the Halifax Port Commission announced the building of a container terminal to use the space.

Work was about to begin on the fourth finger pier, Pier C, of the six announced in 1912, to replace Piers 2 and 3 at Deepwater. That was shelved, but the long-suffering yacht squadron would have to move yet again. They had been at four locations, including the place provided by Samuel Brookfield during the early days of construction. They moved again in May 1971 and went to their current location on the Northwest Arm. They officially opened their new home two months later.[113] The navy vacated the Seaward Defence Base and took over Deepwater Piers 2 and 3, which are now part of the dockyard.

Deepwater was finally gone, after close to a century.

Before the new container terminal could be built, there was the matter of the occupants of the land, who had been there for decades. When the breakwater got finished and the contractors moved to the other end of the development to build the Ocean Terminals docks, the land that had been Miller's Fields, tight against Point Pleasant Park, was vacant. A few workers building the docks had put up temporary shelters in this area, and before long there was a little community near Steele's Pond. By the 1950s there were about forty houses, most owned by the people who lived in them, and the neighbourhood was called Green Bank. Their living was precarious, and, in every sense of the phrase, they were on the wrong side of the tracks—no indoor plumbing, getting water from a single community well, henhouses in the backyard—and they did not own the land on which their houses sat. A tiny corner store, run by Amedée and Stella Marchand, sold the basics. Many decades later, Amedée and Stella's great-grandson, hockey star Brad Marchand, would become the captain of the Boston Bruins before moving to the Florida Panthers and helping his team win his second Stanley Cup.[114]

There was nothing to keep children from wandering around on the more than eighty sets of railway tracks that were just a few metres away. Noise, coal smoke, cinders, and entire trains were ever-present. One resident was railway employee Bill Mont. In 1956, he and his neighbours got a month's notice to vacate the area, which some had labelled

"White Africville," comparing it to the Black community at the other end of the peninsula. The residents of Africville were receiving similar treatment under the pretence that their land was needed for a new bridge across The Narrows. Mont's house was worth $800.

More infilling lay ahead. Excavators and tractors razed the houses and started dumping gravel into the area once occupied by the Seaward Defence Base where Pier C was intended to go. They ended up filling the whole area between Pier B and the breakwater to create two container ship berths and storage space for containers, which had caused transit sheds to become passé. The breakwater got integrated into the dock, and in 2020 the dock was extended still farther out the harbour past the breakwater to create eight hundred metres of continuous berthing space, the most of any port in eastern Canada.

Work also began in the 1970s on a new container terminal to be located in, of all places, Fairview Cove, in the southwest corner of the Bedford Basin, the very location where the naysayers of 1912 claimed they should have developed in the first place. That container terminal opened in 1981. In 2023, Fairview Cove was expanded—thanks to more massive infilling—and doubled its dock space.

Infilling at Ocean Terminals continues in order to expand docking space for more container ships. That's good and bad; good for business but worrying, because there is an incentive to forge ahead with infilling the harbour at a pace limited only by the size and number of the dump trucks beating a path to its shore.

The incentive is a need to dispose of vast amounts of pyritic slate, which is ubiquitous around Halifax. When it is dug up and exposed to air and water, it produces iron oxides, sulphide minerals, and sulphuric acid, which discharge into groundwater and other bodies of water, thus increasing their acidity, making them corrosive and unable to support many forms of aquatic life.

It's a problem because a construction boom in the Halifax area is digging up a lot of this material. It is not as destructive in salt water, so the authorities have decided that the harbour provides a great place to get rid of it, and they are proceeding accordingly. The attitude seems to be that we're blessed with a big harbour, and we need to get rid of this stuff, so...onward! Nobody is asking, "We're covering up centuries of history and making our legendary harbour smaller. Is this a good idea?" Meanwhile, there are landowners up and down the Nova Scotia coast who are prohibited from filling in beside their properties who would gladly take this pyritic slate off the city's hands.

There is a second issue, related to how the people of Halifax suffer because of decisions made elsewhere, just like in 1912. The number of containers going through the port is higher than ever and growing. Halifax's civic infrastructure is groaning under the strain, and the accommodating people of Halifax are losing their patience. Whereas the street closest to the waterfront—Water Street—was once a pleasure to stroll, there are days when it is sheer torture. The roar of eighteen-wheel semi-trailers shuttling containers between the two terminals is ever-present on weekdays and it is often impossible for pedestrians to have a conversation. On the afternoon of July 21, 2025, I decided to stand in one spot and do a count. In thirty-one minutes, twenty-five container-carrying semi-trailers passed by. The thundering engines, the smell of diesel exhaust, the clanging of the machinery: The overwhelming presence of these monsters has made parts of the downtown an awful place to be. With endless construction and the loss of whole traffic lanes to developers' equipment, traffic is often at a standstill. In 2024, tour companies were obliged to refund thousands of dollars to complaining tourists fed up with sitting in traffic when they paid for a tour. Halifax as a tourist destination is getting a bad name.

Is it time for the Ocean Terminals to shut down?

There has been talk of moving the whole container shipping business out of the harbour to another location. One possibility would be Melford in the Strait of Canso, where a 315-acre container terminal and 1,500-acre logistics park have been on the drawing board for about twenty years.

Shutting down the Ocean Terminals would be a bigger change than the original construction had been, but the alternative is to continue with the endless terminal expansions, the ongoing infilling of the harbour, and the incessant transfer of container-carrying eighteen wheelers through the downtown. The job losses would not be large because the whole operation will soon be mechanized anyway.

Piers 20, 21, and 22—the first part of the Ocean Terminals docks to be completed (referred to during construction as the quay)—have also found a new and very successful purpose in hosting cruise ships. The location is ideal, as is the cargo—tourists with money to spend. Travellers step off their ships and find themselves downtown among the historic buildings of old Halifax. The largest cruise ships in the world can tie up. In the same area where the immigrant trains used to board their passengers in the past, buses efficiently receive thousands of visitors and whisk them throughout the city and along the picturesque coast of Nova Scotia. It is common to have eight to ten thousand people arrive, tour, dine, and depart in a single day.

With this activity, the Ocean Terminals have been granted new life. What might have been neglected and deteriorating old buildings atop empty wharves, like in many ports of the world, the steadfast old buildings of the Ocean Terminals ring with life and laughter, bustle and excitement while the world's biggest ships, playfully decorated, decisively and ever-so-slowly crunch the giant fenders against Foley et al.'s sturdy docks as they tie up alongside.

When one stands, on a crisp sunny morning in September, with ships tied at Piers 20 through 23 and thousands of people heading down the gangways and pushing through the security gates into the concourse, then bursting forth to the welcoming outdoors and the dozens of friendly, talkative tour guides waiting to hustle them aboard coaches, double-deckers, minibuses, taxis, and carriages, it's hard to believe that Frederick Cowie and his engineering team did not have this very scene in mind.

It's perfect!

Or is it?

ACKNOWLEDGEMENTS

How shall I describe an archivist? Helpful, patient, and tenacious. And perhaps underappreciated, but not by me!

At the Halifax Municipal Archives, Elena Cremonese, Susan McClure, and Jennifer MacDougall dug out century-old maps, letters, council minutes, photographs, reports, building permits, and a host of other documents that enabled me to slowly piece together this incredible saga.

And the staff at the Nova Scotia Archives have helped me in too many ways to list, as they have for years, from their vast trove of fascinating documents and their great knowledge. In January or February, you can give my ticket to the Caribbean to somebody who will appreciate it. I'll happily spend the two weeks with my friends at the archives.

At the Dalhousie University Archives, not only did Phil Laugher track down a hundred-plus-page thesis but he also scanned it so I could take it home for reference.

My friend Tom Lynskey generously provided many of the key photos of the activity of building the railway cut and the docks.

Kim Batherson of Halifax Grain Elevators Limited spent several hours filling me in with the long story and images of the grain elevator.

And by no means least are a couple of ninety-five-year-olds with enviable memories. Bill Mont can spin yarn after yarn about living in Green Bank and working at the Ocean Terminals. And thanks to my long-time friend Bernie McCorry—ninety-five and irrepressible, and lovingly cared for by his eight daughters—for sharing his reminiscences about the Deep Water Terminus and railway in the 1930s and '40s.

And finally, to Ken Bell for sharing from his experiences building Pier A1 in the 1950s, I am grateful.

APPENDIX A

Expropriation Payments

Well over two hundred properties were expropriated in the course of completing the rail cut. This list is compiled from a variety of archival and newspaper sources. Names that appear multiple times indicate they owned properties at several addresses. The payment column is blank in places where the owner rejected the amount the government offered and was holding out for more or had taken the case to court.

1	Alfred	Thomas	Albert Street	$2,000
2	Miss	Bottomly	Atlantic Street	$1,000
3	Thomas	Bottomly	Atlantic Street	$2,500
4	W. R.	Bryant	Atlantic Street	$500
5	J. E.	Butler	Atlantic Street	$4,200
6	Cyril B.	Clarke	Atlantic Street	
7	Wm.	Fudge	Atlantic Street	$1,000
8	Rev. E.	Gilpin	Atlantic Street	$1,050
9	Sarah	McAulay	Atlantic Street	$2,550
10	Wm.	Murphy	Atlantic Street	$1,000
11	M. A.	Trider	Atlantic Street	
12	A. M.	Bell	Bayers Road	
13	Fairview Cemetery		Bayers Road	
14	St. Paul's Parish		Bayers Road	
15	Capt. John	Hicks	Bower Road	$9,000
16	Capt. John	Hicks	Bower Road	
17	D.	McKeen	Bower Road	
18	W. B. A.	Ritchie	Bower Road	
19	Samuel	Brookfield	Brussels Street	$1,250
20	H.	Roper	Brussels Street	$200

21			Brussels Street	$200
22			Brussels Street	$1,250
23	R. P.	Proctor	Chebucto Road	$15,540
24	John	Miller	Clarence Street	$14,300
25	Birchdale Hotel		Coburg Road	
26	W. T.	Francis	Coburg Road	
27	James	Fraser	Coburg Road	
28	T. E.	Kenny	Coburg Road	$2,000
29	H. P.	Storey	Coburg Road	
30	W. H.	Studd	Coburg Road	
31	Robert	O'Mullin	Coburg Road	$7,500
32	Carritte Patterson & Co.		Dutch Village Road	
33	J. S.	Jones	Dutch Village Road	$2,150
34		Sterling	Dutch Village Road	
35	H.	Blackadar	Fairview, Bedford Road	$300
36	John	Brooks	Fairview, Bedford Road	$7,750
37	John	Brooks	Fairview, Bedford Road	$2,816
38	Albert	Geizer	Fairview, Bedford Road	$6,000
39	J. F.	Gough	Fairview, Bedford Road	$14,250
40	John F.	Gough	Fairview, Bedford Road	$9,000
41	John F.	Gough	Fairview, Bedford Road	$5,000
42	John F.	Gough	Fairview, Bedford Road	$2,650
43	Mrs. V. E.	White	Fairview, Bedford Road	$300

44	Sisters of Charity		Fairview, Bedford Road	
45	Sarah	Fultz	Fawson Street	$3,850
46	Rev. John	McMillan	Fawson Street	$14,000
47	Effie	Oxley	Fawson Street	$7,000
48	Frances	Smith	Fawson Street	$9,000
49	Francis	Smith	Fawson Street	$8,850
50	M. A.	Buckley	Gas Lane	
51	Ellen	Kelly	Gas Lane	$3,000
52	Halifax Electric Tram Co.		Gas Lane	$20,958
53	A. B.	Crosby	Hollis Street	$6,000
54	Mrs.	Johnstone	Hollis Street	$3,500
55	Estate of James	Thomson	Hollis Street	$3,600
56	Kate	Lawson	Jubilee Cottage (Jubilee Road)	$30,000
57	John	Regan	Jubilee Road	
58	Samuel	Brookfield	Marlborough Woods	$1,800
59	Samuel	Brookfield	Marlborough Woods	$1,500
60	C. H.	Cahan	Marlborough Woods	
61	B. F.	Pearson	Marlborough Woods	
62	Misses	Ritchie	Marlborough Woods	
63	Thomas	Brown	Marlborough Woods	$1,500
64	George E.	Nichols	Marlborough Woods	$1,800
65	George E.	Nichols	Marlborough Woods	$1,500
66	Henry	Roper	Marlborough Woods	$2,200
67	A. B.	Hobrecker	Miller Road	$3,000

68	Hon. H. W.	Owen	Miller Subdivision	4,200
69	Dr. J. G.	Bennett	Mumford Road	$4,000
70	St. Patrick's Home		Mumford Road	
71	C. W.	Anderson	NW Arm and Jubilee	$30,000
72	Roderick	Macdonald	Oakland Road	
73	John	Miller	Owen Street	$22,800
74	Trustees of G. T. N.	Miller	Owen Street	$45,000
75	Hon W. H.	Owen	Owen Street	$4,200
76	Sandford	Fleming	Oxford Street	
77	A.	Boutilier	Pleasant Avenue	
78	Charles J.	Bulger	Pleasant Avenue	$2,800
79	N. J.	Lowe	Pleasant Avenue	$3,000
80	Jerusha	McElmon	Pleasant Avenue	$2,400
81	Jerusha	McElmon	Pleasant Avenue	$2,400
82	Mrs. E.	Sutherland	Pleasant Avenue	
83	Mrs. E.	Sutherland	Pleasant Avenue	
84	Frank	Cooke	Pleasant Avenue	$3,250
85	John D.	Dunbrack	Pleasant Avenue	$350
86	Wm.	Dunbrack	Pleasant Avenue	$3,250
87	James E.	Elliott	Pleasant Avenue	$10,982.50
88	Michael	Fripps	Pleasant Avenue	$2,850
89	Frank	Graham	Pleasant Avenue	$4,500
90	Fred	Greenough	Pleasant Avenue	$2,850
91	Isaac	Hiltz	Pleasant Avenue	$3,500
92	Bessie E.	Hart	Pleasant Avenue	$5,000
93	Matilda	Humphries	Pleasant Avenue	$3,050
94	Joseph	Ingraham	Pleasant Avenue	$2,970
95	N. J.	Lowe	Pleasant Avenue	$4,250
96	F. H.	Mathers	Pleasant Avenue	$5,500
97	A. E.	Mitchell	Pleasant Avenue	$4,832

98	Andrew	Mitchell	Pleasant Avenue	$2,970
99	H	Mitchell	Pleasant Avenue	$350
100	Jessie	Naylor	Pleasant Avenue	$4,750
101	Richard	Gillis	Pleasant Avenue	$3,150
102		Wilson Estate	Pleasant Avenue	$30,000
103	Rev. C	Aldrich	Pleasant Street	$1,600
104	Wm.	Barclay	Pleasant Street	$10,632
105	J.	Bauld	Pleasant Street	
106	W. C.	Bauld	Pleasant Street	$9,500
107	R. O. N.	Bayer	Pleasant Street	$10,000
108	F. H.	Bell	Pleasant Street	$12,000
109	A.	Boutilier	Pleasant Street	
110	A.	Boutilier	Pleasant Street	
111	A.	Boutilier	Pleasant Street	
112	A.	Boutilier	Pleasant Street	
113	Samuel	Brookfield	Pleasant Street	$76,500
114	A. H.	Buckley	Pleasant Street	$12,000
115	Margaret	Cahill	Pleasant Street	$9,000
116	Michael	Carney	Pleasant Street	$26,679
117	B. H.	Collins	Pleasant Street	$4,000
118	William	Caul	Pleasant Street	$4,200
119	Helen	Conway	Pleasant Street	$4,500
120	M. Beatrice	Corbett	Pleasant Street	$9,750
121	John	Courtney	Pleasant Street	
122	Sophia	Crane	Pleasant Street	$7,150
123	A. B.	Crosby	Pleasant Street	
124	A. B.	Crosby	Pleasant Street	
125	Elizabeth	Crosskill	Pleasant Street	$5,500
126	Mary Eva	Dunn	Pleasant Street	$6,100
127	Mary	Findlay	Pleasant Street	$4,200
128	Developer Jas	Flinn	Pleasant Street	$5,900
129	Wm.	Gaul	Pleasant Street	$4,200

130	Bessie	Hart	Pleasant Street	$5,000
131	Amelia	Higgs	Pleasant Street	$4,250
132	Estate W.	Jenkins	Pleasant Street	$5,000
133	M. A.	Laidlaw	Pleasant Street	$10,000
134	Neil	Landry	Pleasant Street	$2,985
135	Alex	Love	Pleasant Street	$3,500
136	A. F.	Mackintosh	Pleasant Street	$27,650
137	Mrs. M.	Mason	Pleasant Street	
138	Helen	McGinn	Pleasant Street	$2,800
139	P.	McMullin	Pleasant Street	
140	Robert	Miller	Pleasant Street	$17,000
141	W. H.	Muir	Pleasant Street	$5,700
142	Mary	O'Connor	Pleasant Street	$4,300
143	Ella Y.	Oland	Pleasant Street	
144	Estate	Peters	Pleasant Street	$1,300
145	F. J.	Phelan	Pleasant Street	$12,000
146	Presbyterian Synod Mortgage		Pleasant Street	$5,398.75
147	Mary	Pugh	Pleasant Street	$5,000
148		RNSYS	Pleasant Street	
149	R. H.	Scriven	Pleasant Street	
150	H. R.	Silver	Pleasant Street	$30,000
151	Margaret	Smith	Pleasant Street	$2,500
152	John	Stairs	Pleasant Street	$4,500
153	Annie	Stanford	Pleasant Street	$6,000
154	E. F.	Stevens	Pleasant Street	
155	George E.	Thomas	Pleasant Street	$2,000
156	Alex	Wilson	Pleasant Street	
157	S. Y.	Wilson	Pleasant Street	
158	Mrs. A.	Wright	Pleasant Street	$3,000
159	F.	Bartlaw	Plover Street	$3,000
160	Thomas	Bottomley	Plover Street	$2,800
161	Thomas	Bottomly	Plover Street	
162	Leo	Boudreau	Plover Street	$3,725

163	Samuel	Brookfield	Plover Street	$750
164	G. J.	Burton	Plover Street	$3,500
165	John E.	Chisholm	Plover Street	$3,600
166	Fred	Hall	Plover Street	$3,500
167	Bessie	Hill	Plover Street	$3,000
168	Thomas	Hopper	Plover Street	$2,750
169	J. H.	Kelly	Plover Street	$4,000
170	Florence	Lake	Plover Street	$3,200
171	Amber	Langille	Plover Street	$3,200
172	Thomas F.	McLean	Plover Street	
173	Margaret	Metzler	Plover Street	$1,800
174	Alfred	Payne	Plover Street	$3,500
175	Vincent	Pettipas	Plover Street	$3,100
176	John J.	Quinn	Plover Street	$1,500
177	Henry	Romans	Plover Street	$1,500
178	Henry	Roper	Plover Street	$3,000
179	Mrs. E.	Warry	Plover Street	$3,000
180	Sir Robert	Weatherbee	Plover Street	
181	Estate W. B.	Almon	Pryor Street	$1,575
182	Margaret	Cartile	Purcells Cove Quarry	$600
183	Joseph	Clark	Purcells Cove Quarry	$7,054.76
184	J.	Keefe	Purcells Cove Quarry	$150
185	Charles	Purcell	Purcells Cove Quarry	$600
186	City of Halifax		Quinpool Road	
187	Thomas W	Flinn	Quinpool Road	$26,000
188	Roman Catholic Episcopal Corp.		Quinpool Road	
189	Lady	Thompson	Quinpool Road	$250
190	H. S.	Tremaine	Quinpool Road	$8,600
191	Charles	Tupper	Quinpool Road	

192	W. B.	Wallace	Quinpool Road	$1,250
193	Elizabeth	Houlihan	Skerry Place	$1,500
194	Mary	O'Leary	Skerry Place	$1,300
195	Developer James	Flinn	Skerry Place	$3,000
196	Alex	Wilson	Skerry Place	$2,050
197	A.	Boutilier	South Hollis Street	
198	Mrs. Anna	Cox	South Hollis Street	$2,300
199	Thomas	Doull	South Hollis Street	$1,500
200	Halifax Electric Tramway Co.		South Hollis Street	
201	John	Mahar	South Hollis Street	$3,300
202	Thomas	McCartney	South Hollis Street	$3,900
203	T. P.	McCartney	South Hollis Street	
204	Margaret	McDowell	South Hollis Street	$1,500
205	W. H.	Stevens	South Hollis Street	$6,682
206	Sandford	Fleming	South Street	
207	T. E.	Kenny	South Street	$2,000
208	T. E.	Kenny	South Street	
209	C. C.	Morton	South Street	$6,150
210	Car.	Kirkwood	Tower Road	$6,800
211	Joseph	Outerbridge	Tower Road	$10,000
212	E. D.	Tucker	Tower Road	$10,000
213	B. H.	Collins	Victoria Lane	$800
214	Mrs. Mary	Findlay	Victoria Lane	$4,200
215	H. F.	Heenan	Victoria Lane	$700
216	J. J.	Skerry	Victoria Lane	$282.50

217	W. J.	Thomson	Victoria Lane	$2,500
218	A.	Wilson	Victoria Lane	$1,950
219	A.	Wilson	Victoria Lane	
220	Halifax Electric Tramway Co.		Victoria Lane	
221	A.	Wilson	Victoria Lane	
222	G. S.	Campbell	Young Avenue	
223	Frank	Courtney	Young Avenue	$3,000
224	T. F.	Courtney	Young Avenue	$3,000
225	C. O.	Macdonald	Young Avenue	
226	D. M.	Owen	Young Avenue	$2,500
227	Catherine E.	Ruggles	Young Avenue	$22,800
228	R. P.	Bell		
229	W. A.	Black		
230	R. A.	Brenton		
231		Clayton		
232		Davison		
233		Kendrick		
234	King's Lumber Yard			
235		LeBrock		
236	Katherine	MacDonnell		
237	Edward	Maxwell		
238		Power		

ENDNOTES

1. Frederick W. Cowie, *Report to the Honourable Frank Cochrane on Halifax Harbour* (Ottawa: Canadian Government Railways, July 1, 1913), 22.
2. Quoted by Frederick W. Cowie, *Report to the Honourable Frank Cochrane on Halifax Harbour* (Ottawa: Canadian Government Railways, July 1, 1913), 23.
3. *Halifax Morning Journal*, June 23, 1854.
4. Gordon MacKay Haliburton, "A History of Railways in Nova Scotia" (Master of Arts thesis, Dalhousie University, May 1955), 58.
5. *Halifax Sun*, June 14, 1854.
6. Robert R. Brown, *Bulletin 17*, Canadian Railroad Historical Association (April 15, 1954).
7. *Halifax Herald*, June 6, 1893.
8. L. G. Power, "Statement of the Joint Committee of the City Council and Citizens, upon the Extension of the Intercolonial Railway into the City" (Halifax: March 8, 1875), 11.
9. Harry Chapman, *In the Wake of the Alderney* (Halifax: Nimbus Publishing, 2001), 138–143.
10. Cowie, 23.
11. *Halifax Herald*, October 31, 1912.
12. Ibid.
13. Robert Bruegmann, *Journal of Transport and Land Use* 1, no. 1 (Summer 2008): 6.
14. *Halifax Herald*, October 31, 1912.
15. Ibid., October 16, 1914, p. 2. William Dennis, George S. Campbell, Michael Dwyer, C. H. Mitchell, I. C. Stewart, A. E. Jones, W. A. Black, and John R. McLeod were all "in the know."
16. Ibid., October 31, 1912.
17. Ibid.
18. *Morning Chronicle* (Halifax), November 6, 1912.
19. Ibid., November 9, 1912.
20. Ibid., November 7, 1912.
21. Cowie, 40.
22. Ibid.
23. Ibid., 43.
24. Ibid., 49.
25. *Morning Chronicle* (Halifax), November 1, 1912.
26. Ibid., November 7, 1912.
27. Michael Dwyer in letter to *Morning Chronicle* (Halifax), November 8, 1912.

28. Arthur C. Brown, *Paper #395*, Canadian Society of Civil Engineers, presented April 5, 1917.
29. *Halifax Herald*, November 19, 1912.
30. J. C. Mackintosh, *Halifax Herald*, November 19, 1912.
31. *Morning Chronicle* (Halifax), October 31, 1912.
32. W. A. Henry, K. C., and T. F. Tobin, *Halifax Daily Echo*, November 1, 1912, 2.
33. Steven Schwinghamer and Jan Raska, *Pier 21: A History* (Ottawa: University of Ottawa Press, 2020), 219, n39.
34. *Morning Chronicle* (Halifax), November 7, 1912.
35. "Annual Report of the Halifax Board of Trade," 1911, 65.
36. *Morning Chronicle* (Halifax), November 19, 1912.
37. City of Halifax Council Minutes 1867–1936, July 29, 1913.
38. Murray B. Hodgins, "A City Transformed?: Urban Development and the Role of Canadian Railway Policy in Halifax, Nova Scotia," (Master of Arts thesis, Dalhousie University, 1992), 81.
39. *Morning Chronicle* (Halifax), March 16, 1914.
40. *Halifax Herald*, October 16, 1914, p. 2.
41. City of Halifax Council Minutes 1867–1936, March 27, 1914.
42. *Morning Chronicle* (Halifax), November 4, 1912.
43. *The Novascotian*, September 5, 1913.
44. *Halifax Herald*, June 16, 1913.
45. Douglas N. W. Smith, "The Railways and Canada's Greatest Disaster," *Canadian Rail* no. 431 (November–December 1992), 201.
46. *Morning Chronicle* (Halifax), July 31, 1913.
47. Ibid., August 1, 1913.
48. *Halifax Herald*, June 17, 1913.
49. Fauquier's son, Johnny, was Canada's greatest bomber pilot, with three tours of duty and ninety-three missions. He was the first RCAF officer to lead a bomber squadron and the only Canadian to lead the RAF's elite 617 Squadron, known as the Dam Busters.
50. *Halifax Herald*, July 15, 1914.
51. *Morning Chronicle* (Halifax), November 6, 1912.
52. *Halifax Herald*, August 24, 1916.
53. Petition of Young Avenue residents, *Morning Chronicle* (Halifax), March 25, 1914.
54. Hodgins, 102.
55. Letter from FWW Doane to Mayor F. P. Bligh, Municipal Archives Board of Control Submissions, RG 3-102 Series 2B, November 10, 1913.
56. Letter from Andrew Wheaton to Mayor F. P. Bligh, Municipal Archives Board of Control Submissions, RG 3-102 Series 2B, February 10, 1914.
57. *Halifax Herald*, August 4, 1913.
58. *Morning Chronicle* (Halifax), January 26, 1914.
59. Board of Control Minutes, RG 3-102 Series 2B, January 28, 1914, 694–5.
60. Ibid.

61. Board of Control Submissions.
62. Ibid.
63. City of Halifax Council Minutes, RG 3-102 Series 2B, 222.
64. Letter from Fred Pearson to Mayor F. P. Bligh, Municipal Archives, RG 3-102 Series 2B, August 17, 1914.
65. *Halifax Herald*, August 24, 1916.
66. *Halifax Herald & Morning Chronicle* (Halifax), October 19, 1916.
67. Letter from Andrew Wheaton to Halifax City Clerk Fred Monahan, July 15, 1915.
68. As this is based on surviving documents, it should not be inferred that these are the only exchanges that occurred on the subject. They probably talked, and some documents may no longer exist.
69. Brown, *Paper #395*.
70. Board of Control Minutes, May 23, 1913, 50.
71. Ibid., February 4, 1916, 677.
72. Ibid., May 31, 1916, 84.
73. Ross & Macdonald would go on to design the Hydrostone district of Halifax following the Halifax Explosion.
74. Board of Control Minutes, March 16, 1917, 804.
75. Ibid., July 25, 1916, 216.
76. Ibid., August 2, 1916, 247–8.
77. "Annual Report of the Halifax Board of Trade," 1913, 57.
78. "Halifax, the National Mail Port," *Morning Chronicle*, January 22, 1914.
79. "The Mail Question in a Nutshell," *Morning Chronicle*, January 23, 1914.
80. *Halifax Herald*, May 20, 1895.
81. Ibid., June 16, 1913.
82. Stephen J. Thorne, "My great-uncle William was killed in the attack on Regina Trench," *Legion Magazine*, July 8, 2001. legionmagazine.com/hit-so-soon/.
83. *Halifax Herald*, August 24, 1916.
84. *Halifax Herald*, September 28, 1916.
85. "Ocean Terminals History," *Halifax Herald*, December 31, 1917.
86. Ibid.
87. Thomas H. Raddall, *Halifax: Warden of the North* (Toronto: McClelland and Stewart, 1971), 259.
88. F. B. Tapley, "Salvaging the Railway Facilities at Halifax, Nova Scotia," *Railway Age* 64, no. 20 (May 17, 1918). archives.novascotia.ca/macmechan/archives/?ID=35&Page=201761293.
89. *Canadian Rail Magazine*, no. 431 (November–December 1992): 209.
90. Ibid., 212.
91. Ibid., 210.
92. *Halifax Herald*, December 23, 1918.
93. *Halifax Herald*, April 11, 1914.
94. *Halifax Herald*, December 23, 1918.
95. J. S. Scott, "A Monument to the Persistence of a National Spirit," *Port and Province*, December 1934, 9.
96. *Halifax Herald*, August 24, 1916.

97. Schwinghamer and Raska., *Pier 21: A History*, 61.
98. Ibid.
99. Ibid.
100. *Halifax Herald*, December 31, 1917.
101. *Port and Province*, Sept.–Oct. 1934, 8.
102. *Halifax Mail-Star*, October 10, 1953.
103. *Halifax Mail-Star*, November 25, 1964, and September 21, 1965.
104. *Halifax Herald*, February 28, 1928.
105. Ibid.
106. *Halifax Herald*, March 12, 1928.
107. Notice in *Halifax Chronicle*, July 7, 1927.
108. Brown, *Paper #395*, 265.
109. *Halifax Herald*, October 15, 1927.
110. Ibid., June 25, 1930.
111. *Port and Province*, December 1934, 10.
112. *The Crowsnest* 6, no. 2 (December 1953): 6.
113. Nancy Erhard, First in Its Class: *The Story of the Royal Nova Scotia Yacht Squadron* (Halifax: Nimbus Publishing, 1986), 128.
114. *Frank Magazine*, August 30, 2011, 12.
115. Henry Roper, "The Halifax Board of Control: The Failure of Municipal Reform, 1906–1919," *Acadiensis* 14, no. 2 (1985): 54.
116. *Halifax Herald*, September 28, 1916.
117. Ibid., June 24, 1930.

BIBLIOGRAPHY

"Annual Reports" of the Halifax Board of Trade.

Brown, Arthur C. *Paper #395.* Canadian Society for Civil Engineering, presented April 5, 1917.

Brown, Robert R. *Bulletin 17,* Canadian Railroad Historical Association, Montréal, April 15, 1954.

The Canadian Annual Review of Public Affairs 1925–26. Toronto: The Canadian Review.

Chapman, Harry. *In the Wake of the Alderney.* Halifax: Nimbus Publishing, 2001.

Cowie, Frederick W. *Report to the Honourable Frank Cochrane on Halifax Harbour.* Ottawa: Canadian Government Railways, July 1, 1913.

Cunningham, Don, and Don Artz. *The Halifax Street Railway.* Halifax: Nimbus Publishing, 2009.

Doane, FWW. "History of the Halifax Rifles Regiment 1888 1934," unpublished.

Erhard, Nancy. *First in Its Class: The Story of the Royal Nova Scotia Yacht Squadron.* Halifax: Nimbus Publishing, 1986.

Haliburton, Gordon MacKay. *A History of Railways in Nova Scotia.* Master of Arts Thesis, Dalhousie University, May 1955.

Hodgins, Murray B. "A City Transformed? Urban Development and the Role of Canadian Railway Policy in Halifax, Nova Scotia." Master of Arts Thesis, Dalhousie University, 1992.

Hopper, A. B., and T. Kearney. "Canadian National Railways Synoptical History of Organization, Capital Stock, Funded Debt and Other General Information." Montréal: CNR Accounting Department, 1962.

MacKenzie, Shelagh. *Halifax Street Names*. Halifax: Formac Publishing, 2002.

McAlpine Halifax City Directories 1910 through 1920. Halifax: McAlpine Publishing.

Millington, Elsie. *Purcell's Cove: The Little Place that Helped Build Halifax City*. Halifax: Self-published, 2000.

Halifax Board of Control, "Meeting Minutes."

Halifax City Council, "Meeting Minutes."

Halifax Field Naturalists Newsletter, No. 26, April–December 1981.

Halifax Registry of Deeds.

House of Commons Debates, 12th Parliament, 2nd Session: Vol 6.

Power, L. G. "Statement of the Joint Committee of the City Council and Citizens, upon the Extension of the lntercolonial Railway into the City." Halifax, March 8, 1875.

Raddall, Thomas H. *Halifax: Warden of the North*. Toronto: McClelland and Stewart, 1971.

Regan, John W. *Sketches and Traditions of the Northwest Arm*. Willowdale: Hounslow Press, 1978.

Schwinghamer, Steven, and Jan Raska. *Pier 21: A History*. Ottawa: University of Ottawa Press, 2020.

Smith, Douglas N. W. "The Railways and Canada's Greatest Disaster." *Canadian Rail* 431. St. Constant, QC, November–December 1992.

Stephens, David E, *Iron Roads: Railways of Nova Scotia*. Windsor, NS: Lancelot Press, 1972.

Tapley, F. B. "Salvaging the Railway Facilities at Halifax, Nova Scotia." *Railway Age* 64, no. 20. Chicago: Simmons-Boardman Publishing, May 17, 1918.

Watts, Heather, and Michelle Raymond. *Halifax's Northwest Arm*. Halifax: Formac Publishing, 2003.

Newspapers and Periodicals

Acadiensis

British Colonist

Canadian Rail

Commercial News

Crowsnest

Daily Acadian Recorder

Daily Echo

Daily News

Frank Magazine

Halifax Herald

Halifax Sun

Journal of Transport and Land Use

Legion Magazine

Morning Chronicle (Halifax)

Morning Journal

Novascotian

Port and Province

Railway Age

Unionist

ALSO BY BOB CHAULK

978-1-77471-010-4

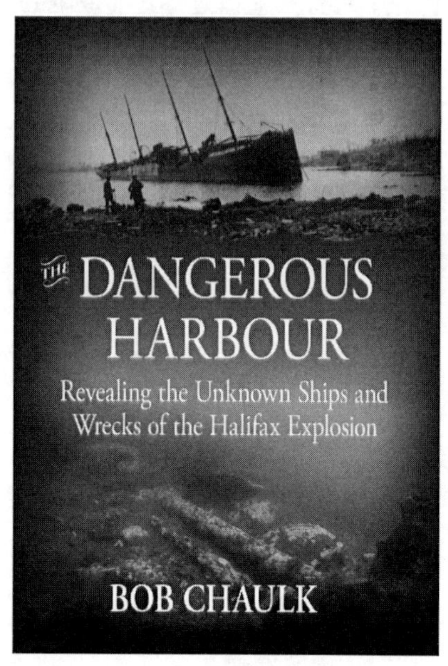

978-1-77471-240-5